Praise for *Liquid Gold*

'A great book. Painstakingly researched, but humorous, sensitive and full of wisdom. I'm on the verge of getting some bees as a consequence of reading the book.'

CHRIS STEWART, author of *Driving Over Lemons*

'Beekeeping builds from lark to revelation in this carefully observed story of midlife friendship. Filled with humour and surprising insight, *Liquid Gold* is as richly rewarding as its namesake. Highly recommended.'

THOR HANSON, author of *Buzz: The Nature and Necessity of Bees*

'*Liquid Gold* is a book that ignites joy and warmth through a layered and honest appraisal of beekeeping. Roger Morgan-Grenville deftly brings to the fore the fascinating life of bees but he also presents in touching and amusing anecdotes the mind-bending complexities and frustrations of getting honey from them. But like any well-told story from time immemorial, he weaves throughout a silken thread, a personal narrative that is at once self-effacing, honest and very human. In this book you will not only meet the wonder of bees but the human behind the words.'

MARY COLWELL, author of *Curlew Moon*

LIQUID GOLD

BEES AND THE PURSUIT OF MIDLIFE HONEY

ROGER MORGAN-GRENVILLE

ICON

Published in the UK and USA in 2020
by Icon Books Ltd, Omnibus Business Centre,
39–41 North Road, London N7 9DP
email: info@iconbooks.com
www.iconbooks.com

Sold in the UK, Europe and Asia
by Faber & Faber Ltd, Bloomsbury House,
74–77 Great Russell Street,
London WC1B 3DA or their agents

Distributed in the UK, Europe and Asia
by Grantham Book Services,
Trent Road, Grantham NG31 7XQ

Distributed in the USA
by Publishers Group West,
1700 Fourth Street, Berkeley, CA 94710

Distributed in Canada by Publishers Group Canada,
76 Stafford Street, Unit 300
Toronto, Ontario M6J 2S1

Distributed in Australia and New Zealand
by Allen & Unwin Pty Ltd,
PO Box 8500, 83 Alexander Street,
Crows Nest, NSW 2065

Distributed in South Africa
by Jonathan Ball, Office B4, The District,
41 Sir Lowry Road, Woodstock 7925

Distributed in India by Penguin Books India,
7th Floor, Infinity Tower – C, DLF Cyber City,
Gurgaon 122002, Haryana

ISBN: 978-178578-605-1

Text copyright © 2020 Roger Morgan-Grenville

The author has asserted his moral rights.

Typeset in Sabon by Marie Doherty

Printed and bound in Great Britain
by Clays Ltd, Elcograf S.p.A.

CONTENTS

ABOUT THE AUTHOR

Roger Morgan-Grenville was a soldier in the Royal Green Jackets from 1978–1986, serving all over the world. In 1984–85, he led the first expedition that successfully retraced Sir Ernest Shackleton's escape across the sub-Antarctic island of South Georgia. After leaving the British army, he worked in, and then ran, a small family company importing and selling kitchenware. In 2007–08, he helped to set up the charity Help for Heroes, acting as its first head fundraiser and volunteer coordinator. He jointly set up a roving cricket team in 1986 (The White Hunters) and lives in West Sussex. This is his fourth book.

To my parents, who gave me so many opportunities to love nature.

DISCLAIMER

Beekeeping has inherent risks due to the toxicity of bee stings. If you are stung by a bee and experience symptoms such as difficulty in breathing, swelling of the tongue and throat, and/or a weak, rapid pulse, or you feel unwell in any way, seek immediate medical advice. Any adverse reaction to a bee sting, or multiple bee stings, should be taken seriously and referred to a medical professional before continuing with beekeeping activities.

The contents of this book do not constitute professional advice on beekeeping. Neither the author nor the publisher shall be liable or responsible for any loss or damage allegedly arising from any information or suggestion contained in this book.

A NOTE ON NAMES

Some of the names of people, places and organisations in this book have been changed to protect their privacy and anonymity, and to avoid invading the quiet spaces of people doing what is essentially a peaceful hobby.

PROLOGUE

1969

He was called Mr Fowler.

Like most children then, I lived in a world devoid of adult first names, and so Mr Fowler he stayed. And when I thought of him, I really only thought of him as Mr McGregor in Beatrix Potter's *The Tale of Peter Rabbit*. All I remember about him now is that he had a flat cap that he never took off, and a pipe that he never took out of his mouth.

He gardened for my grandfather, which must have been no mean feat, as my grandfather was a formidable gardener himself. One midsummer afternoon, while I was staying, I tiptoed round to the greenhouse to help myself to a couple of his Gardener's Delight tomatoes while no one was looking, only to find that Mr Fowler *was* looking. He was there in the shadows, operating the antique watering system, but he was forgiving enough to hand me a couple to try, anyway. Perfectly did he understand the elemental pleasure of the smell and taste of an old-fashioned tomato straight off the vine in a hot greenhouse. For a minute or two, he stood with me watching a bee hard at work on the flowers above.

'Why's it doing that?' I asked him as it darted from flower to flower as if its life depended on it.

'It's not an "it",' he said sternly. 'It's a she. And she's foraging. She's collecting pollen and nectar to take back to the hive to turn into honey.'

'How does she do that?' I asked, chastened. In the monochrome world of 1960s food, honey was something I actually liked and could easily identify with.

'With a lot of help from her friends,' he answered, and went back to his work on the stirrup pump. He wasn't paid to entertain nine-year-old boys.

Mr Fowler kept a hive himself, in his little plot a couple of miles away. At some stage, he must have spoken to my grandfather about my furtive visit to the greenhouse, as the next time I went round, the latter announced that I had been invited over to the Fowlers' for tea, and that I would be shown the hive if I was very good and said please and thank you to Mrs Fowler at all the right times.

So, when he had finished his day's work, Mr Fowler and I bundled wordlessly back through the shady chestnut lane in his pale green Hillman Imp. As soon as we arrived at his cottage he became as light and frivolous as he had been stern and grave in my grandparents' garden, as if the act of removing his hat and revealing the previously unseen bald head had lifted all formality from him. He and Mrs Fowler fussed over me like the sweet old people I'd only ever read about in Enid Blyton books, plying me with sandwiches, cake and lemonade, telling me that I would never grow to be a big lad unless I kept eating and eating. At length, Mr Fowler put his hat back on and led me down the side of his tiny garden, to a spot by a bank on the edge of the neighbouring farmland.

'There you are,' he said. 'That's a beehive. Do you want to look inside it?'

I wasn't entirely sure that I did, now that I was close up. But, after that huge tea and with a modicum of childish intuition, I understood that 'no' wasn't on the menu of acceptable answers.

'Oh, yes please!' I said.

So he went back to his shed and brought out two faded white hats with veils attached, and a single pair of gloves. Having got my hat on, and with my veil securely tucked into the top of my sweater, and my trousers stuffed into my boots, I was still alarmed that he had only one pair of gloves.

'A proper beekeeper doesn't use gloves,' he said, beaming. 'He needs to feel how the bees are behaving, and he can't do that through leather, or even cotton. Here, these are for you. Shall we open it up now?'

He lit a little bee smoker, and directed a few puffs into the hole at the bottom of the hive.

'Why do you do that?' I asked, sniffing at the wreaths of burned cardboard smoke that filtered up into the summer air.

'That just calms them,' he explained.

I'm not sure what I was expecting to see as he took the roof off the hive and laid it carefully on the ground – but, for a second or two, I was close to sheer panic. I had never seen so many living things in one place, so pulsating with hidden energy, and so densely packed. The impression of a chaos so much vaster than me made me slightly nauseous. The top of the open box revealed a moving carpet of bees, writhing this way and that, and rising and falling. I had recently read T.H. White's *The Sword in the Stone*, and all I knew about insects came from the few pages when Merlin turns Wart into an ant, and that had frightened rather than helped. A few bees flew at my veil, and I could hear the angry buzz of their wings, beating 200 times to the second. I had been stung by bees before, and the multiplied thought that there were maybe 50,000 of them in this box brought me up short for a second or two. I drew back a couple of paces, scared of being seen to be scared, but wary of being too close.

'Don't worry about the bees,' said Mr Fowler, taking two smaller boxes off the big one at the bottom. 'If you keep calm, they won't bother you. And anyway, you're well protected.'

With his bare hands and a prong from his gardener's penknife, he levered the frames free from where wax and honey had stuck them to the box, and showed them to me as he took each one out to inspect it. I watched a few bees crawling across the backs of his hands, and wondered if he, too, was a bit nervous but just didn't want to show it to a boy like me. Pointing at how the queen had laid eggs all around the drawn-out wax foundation, he showed me the difference between new brood and sealed brood, and explained what the significance of each was. On the fourth or fifth frame, he said excitedly:

'Look! There she is! There's our queen!' And, where he was pointing, squirming her way through a seething mass of bees around her was, indeed, one that was nearly twice the size and marked with a big red dot on her back. When I asked him how many queens there were in the hive, he said: 'Only one! Just like Her Majesty in London. Just the one.'

'But there's no honey,' I said. Honey was really why I was here.

He had been waiting for the question. 'That's because most of the honey's in the smaller boxes. Don't worry, we'll have a look when we've finished inspecting this one.'

'Why's there no honey in the big box?' I asked, and he said patiently that there *was* a bit, but that this was a lesson for another day.

Once the last frame was back in the box, he laid the first smaller box back on top of it, and pulled out a frame from that one to show me. It was glistening with honey, rich, golden honey in every available nook and cranny, as far as I could see. He handed the frame to me and asked me with a serious expression whether I thought we were ready for the harvest.

'Oh yes!' I said. 'I think we're ready.'

'Well, I'll tell you what. When you next come and see your grandpa, be sure he tells me that you're coming. Then you can come here as well and help me take the honey.'

After a few more minutes, he reassembled the component parts and closed up the hive.

'What will the bees do if we take all their honey? Isn't it what keeps them alive in the winter?'

He explained briefly that he gave them other food like sugar syrup, and that they were happy enough with that.

'I wouldn't be happy if you took away all my honey and just gave me sugar. Not at all.' A tiny and indignant part of me was fighting for the bees, and he surprised me by saying quietly that perhaps I had a point.

'Think you could make a beekeeper?' he asked, as we walked the path back to his house, where my grandfather had recently arrived and was talking to Mrs Fowler.

'Oh yes!' I said. But it was more to show enthusiasm for a pot of his honey than any wish to be involved again with that maelstrom of uncontrolled energy inside a hive. Boys of nine don't easily understand when they are being honoured.

'Don't forget to come again!' he called out to us as we drove away.

But I never did. The summer became autumn, and the autumn became a new year that brought with it different enthusiasms, coupled with the wish to share them with boys of my own age rather than old countrymen like Mr Fowler.

Anyway, within a year he was cold in the clay himself, taken in his garden one sunny afternoon by a heart attack, and it was too late to ask.

I like to think he was with his bees at the end.

Chapter 1

THE BEGINNINGS

May

....

I believe that life is chaotic, a jumble of
accidents, ambitions, misconceptions,
bold intentions, lazy happenstances
and unintended consequences, yet I
also believe that there are connections
that illuminate our world, revealing
its endless mystery and wonder.

DAVID MARANISS

....

It was a windy day in May, with heavy showers running along the line of the South Downs.

Lunch was over, the coffee drunk, and we were wondering whether to offer to help wash up or just to head home and let our friends get on with it. The idea had originally been for the four of us to go for a walk with the dogs in the afternoon, but the appetite for it had been washed away by the regular rain. I saw Jim standing by the window, staring out across the garden into the field beyond.

'That's the third this week,' he said, almost under his breath.

'Third what?'

He seemed momentarily surprised by the question. 'Third swarm of bees,' he said. 'I don't think I saw a single one last year, but this time they're everywhere.'

I joined him at the window, and looked out at what appeared to be a rugby ball hanging off a low branch of a nearby cedar tree. I had seen bees swarming before, but I had never really noticed a swarm settling like this. Jim said it was smaller than the two he had seen earlier in the week, and that it would probably soon be gone.

'Where do they come from?' I asked.

'Could be anywhere.' But he explained that their neighbour had kept two hives in his garden for years, and that he had left his wife a few months before, and there was probably no one looking after them any more.

'It might be them,' he said. 'Equally, they are rather more likely to be from a wild colony somewhere deep in a hollowed-out tree, or up in the gap behind the eaves of a building. This is just what they do.'

It had never really occurred to me to wonder what bees did, or why they did it. I had once seen into a glass-backed hive in a local museum when I was a child, but I had long since forgotten whatever I had learned there. And, of course, I had seen Mr Fowler's bees, although that was nearly half a century ago: 500 generations of honeybees would have come and gone since then. Nowadays, I only saw bees buzzing from plant to plant in my garden. I also read articles about the decline in their numbers, and what would happen to us all if their numbers fell below a certain tipping point.

'Swarming is the only way they can reproduce their colonies.' We were still staring out of the window at the dark lump hanging off the cedar. 'Basically, they are only meant to have one queen until, one day, something tells the workers to create another one. That's where it all starts.'

'How do you know all this?' I asked. This was as talkative as he ever got. Normally, Jim's style was to just sit and listen to the noise of the world around him.

'Oh, I kept a couple of hives for years. Ever since I was a boy, actually. Found them on the farm when we moved in, and got them going again.' He told me that he had given up only when they had discovered that one of their young children had developed an allergic reaction to bee stings, and to continue with the hobby would just be tempting fate. One of the hives had already been empty, and he had given the other one away, complete with its contents, to a teacher at the local primary school.

'I think there's a number we're meant to call for the local beekeepers' association, so that one of them comes and takes the swarm. That way, you get rid of the bees, and they get a brand-new colony for free. But I reckon they'll be gone soon, so I'll just leave them to it.'

'Why don't I take them?'

I can't remember actually saying it, but Jim assures me I did. For at least the next eighteen months, I would ask myself from which part of my brain that comment had come.

'You haven't got the kit, and you wouldn't know what to do with it if you did. Apart from that, there's nothing to stop you.' He continued to gaze out at the swarming bees in his garden.

Then after a while, and with no further prompting from me, he said: 'I suppose we could just take it, and see what happened.'

So we went out across Jim's small farmyard to a shed that was full of terracotta flowerpots and old rolls of chicken wire, and found the redundant beekeeping kit high up on a wide shelf in the far, dark corner.

'Look!' he said, beaming with pleasure, 'My old beekeeping suit.' Every variety of British moth seemed to have had a go at it in the years it had been up there but it was still just about recognisable as the top half of a bee suit with an inbuilt veil. Then he chucked down some gloves, a filthy old sheet and a strangely shaped steel tool with flakes of yellow paint on it. It was a barn – indeed it was a farm – where stuff arrived and never left.

'Have you got a smoker?' I remembered Mr Fowler all those years ago, and that smell of burning cardboard.

'Not needed. Once we get a strong cardboard box and some clippers, we're done,' he said, and led me back out into the drizzle to collect his old hive and put it, disassembled, into the boot of my car.

'But there's two of us, and we only have one suit,' I complained, as we approached the bees. In my mind's eye, I was going to be the one who stood back and offered encouraging words from a safe distance. This was a job for experts.

'I never said that *I* would do it, only that I would enable *you* to do it. It's your show, but once you're down there it will be a piece of cake. And anyway, swarming bees are incredibly docile, as they aren't defending their honey.' He looked rather pleased with himself at this observation.

A few yards from the tree, I put on the bee suit, which smelled of old paint and decay, tucked my trousers into my socks and listened to his explanation of how to go about it.

'It's simple. Get the bees off that branch by cutting it, and get them into the box. So long as you have the queen, the others will follow after a few minutes. If you're still missing loads of them, just put the box upside down with a small gap at the bottom of one side so that the absentees can come in. Then wrap the box up with the sheet, knot it, and go home.'

'Wouldn't it be easier if you did it this time round?' I was suddenly regretting the wine I had drunk at lunch, and the ridiculous idea that I could become an opportunist beekeeper. This needed the professionals.

'I've never done it before either,' said Jim, explaining that he had *seen* it done, and felt that this should be quite sufficient briefing for me to proceed. His place was watching from the dry, warm kitchen with his hands round a large mug of tea.

'But apparently it's all about smell,' he added, as he headed back up to the house.

So there I was in a wet field on a Sunday afternoon, half-protected by a beekeeping suit that was riddled with holes, and armed with a damp cardboard box, a dust sheet, and a pair of secateurs. I glanced back at the kitchen window where Jim had taken up residence once again. He had been joined by his wife and mine, the latter looking disappointingly unconcerned.

Only some months later did it start to dawn on me just how I had arrived in that wet field, how such tiny substitutions of unplanned adventure had tended to seep into a middle life that had become, in itself, all too planned. Where Jim had seen a swarm of bees hanging off the lower branches of a cedar tree as a little feature of natural history, I had seen it simply as an opportunity, something new in a life that had too little new in it, something a tiny bit risky in a life predominantly safe. I had no real intention of doing anything more than seeing if I could take a swarm of bees without instruction. Mine was an intervention that had no plan beyond walking into a large group of stinging insects and seeing what happened.

The swarm and I watched each other from a suitable distance for a while, a handful of bees flying over curiously to check me out. Step by step I approached the cedar tree and, as I got nearer, I realised that two things were wrong. First, the branch was far too thick for the secateurs to cut through; and, secondly, that I really didn't have the faintest clue about what was going to happen. I stretched my gloved hand up to the top of the mass of the swarm and, for a moment, it seemed Jim was right: beyond a little local agitation, they really didn't appear to mind me being around. Everything depended on what I did next.

In the textbooks, what I did next should probably not have been accidentally to drop the secateurs into the middle of the swarm while I was trying to hack away at the branch. About 25,000 bees rose angrily up in the air, and I got my first sting of the afternoon for my troubles, before they settled back around the branch again. My sweater had become untucked from the glove on the left hand, and a quarter of an inch is plenty of available skin for *Apis mellifera* to home in on. I wanted to rub my hand, but I wanted more not to give the audience any idea that the operation wasn't going perfectly. I looked up at the window and saw Jim bringing his right fist down into his cupped left hand, and worked out after a bit that he was suggesting I just bashed the whole lot of them off the branch and into the box below.

When I first tried this, a disappointingly small percentage of the bees fell off the branch and into the box, and the violence of the action only led them to become angrier and more active. However, it also meant that I was by now fully committed, and so I hurriedly started to brush swathes of bees into the box with my forearm. It wasn't perfect, but after a minute or so I had more bees inside the box than outside, with the rest of the swarm flying angrily around me. It wasn't what I had envisaged at the outset, but it was just about possible to imagine that I could have them all settled in another quarter of an hour. I carefully put the box on the unfolded sheet on the damp grass, turned it upside down and wedged a small stick under one side to leave a gap for the others to come in. Everything now depended on whether I had got the queen on the first run. If I had, they would come; if I hadn't, then it was all over.

While I was watching, and starting to realise with a measure of satisfaction that the direction of travel was *into* the box, not out of it, I also noticed that I was no longer alone in my veil. Two bees had joined me inside it, a fact I worked out by being able to see their backs, rather than their undersides. This is not a good feeling for any beekeeper, and it seemed pretty obvious that it wasn't going to end well for either me or my new friends. The fact that I couldn't see how they had got in indicated that I therefore wouldn't be able to find a way of getting them out, and so I just got on with what I was doing, and waited for the inevitable. Sting number two, when it came, was on my scalp, and sting number three followed shortly afterwards on the side of my neck. Idly, my brain, part of which was involved in starting to close up the box now that the flow of bees into it was drying up, was calculating the time it would take to drive down to the Accident & Emergency department at St Richard's Hospital on a wet Sunday afternoon, if it all went wrong.

An early word on stings.

Two things, unfortunately, define bees in the mind of the disinterested observer: honey and being stung. From earliest childhood, our minds are allowed to bundle the honeybee into a huge category of annoying and potentially dangerous insects that we should avoid, and consequently not care about. This mindset has a profound effect on our attitude to them through childhood and beyond, a situation that has not worked to the bee's advantage.

Bees are passive creatures, and only sting when their hive or honey is threatened, or if they are being roughly handled. Most bees die after stinging a human (the barbed sting is ripped away along with half her abdomen as she flies off), so it is not an action that nature encourages them to do other than *in extremis*.

Beekeepers, even the very best ones, will get stung from time to time. They just will. So long as the actual sting is removed without delay, the pain, which is a result of the apitoxin that has been injected, will subside reasonably quickly, and the swelling within 24 hours. You can take your pick from a thousand traditional cures for a sting, including garlic, copper, toothpaste and prayer, but I have found that time, plus anything with benzocaine in it, kills off the pain. The one old wives' tale I have found to be completely true, is that the melittin within the sting has a short-lived, but nonetheless profound, effect on stiff joints in the area of the sting; unsurprisingly, Californians now pay a great deal of money to get themselves stung. In both senses of the word. To be fair, if a bee were taking part in this conversation, she would add that their produce arguably offers ten health benefits for humans to the one disadvantage they themselves bring. These run from protection against cancer to sugar regulation, anti-bacterial effects, skin care and sorting out coughs, and there is some evidence to back these up. However, there is a lot more evidence to suggest that you should avoid getting stung when you can.

A very small percentage of people develop a hypersensitivity after one sting which can lead to a severe anaphylactic shock when stung again later. This is one of the main reasons that many beekeepers give up the hobby, and therefore it is also a more than adequate source of cheap second-hand equipment on eBay. Most beekeepers await the first sting of a new season with keen interest, as that is the one that will likely reveal if any sensitivity within their bodies has changed.

Over time, I have come to regard a successful season as one where pots of honey harvested outnumber stings received by a factor of twelve to one, or better.

But back on that wet Sunday in May, I knew nothing about bee stings other than that they hurt, and that they prevented me from getting on with what I was trying to achieve. It had probably been half an hour since I had first approached the swarm, but there was now only sporadic activity around the box, and a quiet if rather sinister hum coming from within it. I decided that this was as good as it was going to get, and carefully wrapped the box in the sheet before knotting it up and carrying it back to my car. I allowed myself a faint pulse of pride for not entirely messing this up. I may well have been soaked, dirty and in pain, but I had also kick-started a new adventure, however short it might turn out to be – and new adventures, I was to discover, are the tiny building blocks of middle life.

It took a little bit of persuasion to get Jim to temporarily part with all his beekeeping kit, and rather more to get Caroline to climb into a car that now contained up to 30,000 new house guests.

'You'll be fine. They're in a box, in a sheet, knotted up and completely safe.'

'But what are you going to do with them when you get them home?' she asked.

Caroline is a graduate in physiology, an achievement that combines with her natural persistence to give her an unfortunate habit of asking practical questions at inconvenient times.

'I have a plan,' I replied, as if my secret confidence settled the matter. I didn't tell her that my plan simply consisted of doing an internet search on 'what to do with 30,000 bees' and then following whatever instruction it gave. I also didn't tell her, of more immediate concern, that I had spotted two or three bees rising up in the rear-view mirror, where they definitely should not have been. I opened the windows in the hope that the rush of air would pin them against the back windscreen and leave them undetected.

'Can we stop for some milk?' she asked, as we drove through the local town.

'I'll nip back and get some later,' I said.

'But why not do it now, while we're outside the shop?'

I looked nervously in the mirror, where a few more bees had emerged. Knowing that things could get quite awkward quite quickly, I said something about the bees needing to be settled down as soon as possible, and stamped on the accelerator for the five-mile journey home. By the time we got there, there were possibly 30 bees flying around the box in the back of the car, looking for all the world like latecomers to a rock festival.

Garbage in, as they say, garbage out.

The quality of the answer that you get from a search engine depends entirely on the question you pose in the first place. Having secured the box of bees with a tighter knot, and left it in the shelter of the porch, I went to my computer and asked it 'how to rehome a swarm of bees'. The subsequent articles I speed-read, and videos that I watched, all came from the start point that the person asking this question a) was a beekeeper and b) had a working hive and all the necessary equipment to go with it. I had been a beekeeper since about 3.30pm, and all I had was an unassembled hive in the back of my car that was in the latter stages of decay. There was an entire new glossary of words and terms that I had never come across, each of which needed to be deciphered before I could make progress with the basic instruction I was being given. On YouTube, all the videos were either of suspiciously calm bees doing exactly what their people wanted, or of drawling Alabaman hill farmers in checked shirts who called their bees 'critters', which made them impossible to take seriously.

Gradually, I learned that there were two basic ways to rehome bees in a new hive: lay a white sheet up a plank that leads from your box to the entry hole of the hive, and wait for them to find, and then occupy, their new home; or just open the lid of the hive and dump them in. The article that put me on to this explained that the first of these methods is the most natural and stress-free for the bees, and so I chose it. If I was going to make it as a contributor to, and beneficiary from, this strange new world, then it had to be done in a way that respected my guests; there would be no rude dumping of bees into a hive on my honey farm.

Telling the box that I would 'be back soon' as I passed it at the front door, I headed off to set up the hive in the most suitable place I could find in my garden, a small corner between the compost heap and the oil tank that was sheltered from rain, wind and sun. I cleared some long grass, then started what I assumed would be the straightforward task of assembling the hive itself. Suddenly I was in a new and entirely esoteric world of brood boxes, stands, crown boards and queen excluders, with little idea of what they did, and even less of where they went. Being someone with all the fine motor skills of a blue whale, I desperately needed someone's help at the same time as not wanting to admit to that someone that I hadn't got a clue what I was doing. However, by degrees I worked out which bit went on which other, and eventually had something on my hands that looked close to, if not exactly like, the hives I had seen. It may have had all the allure of a condemned tenement block, but it had a roof, and it had stuff in it, which for the time being was good enough for me.

Triumphantly, I went back to the house and took a clean white sheet out of the airing cupboard while Caroline wasn't looking. I wanted my bees to feel like honoured guests in their new home, and there is nothing, as I saw it, quite like the feel of Egyptian cotton to create a first impression of luxury and well-being. I wasn't sure that she would see things in the same way, and opted for the tried and tested maxim that it is normally easier in life to apologise retrospectively than to ask permission.

I put on the veil again, picked up the box and headed back with my guests to their new home. The way I saw it, short of candle-lit tables and a Michelin-starred chef preparing a meal for them, I couldn't have done much more to make them feel welcome. The only fly in the ointment was the rain, which now looked like it had set in for the evening. If I was expecting a burst of activity and noise as I carefully untied the knot in the sheet and started to open the box, I was to be sorely disappointed. They were all down at the bottom of the box looking out of sorts and lethargic, a mindset that would surely change as they became aware of their new, luxurious surroundings. Slowly, I turned the box upside down and shook its contents down onto the crisp white sheet below.

'It's up to you now, guys,' I told them cheerfully. 'Get in there quickly before the rain really sets in.'

Once back in the house, I continued my research with diligence and, gradually, the whole hidden, secret, magical, beautiful world of the honeybee started to reveal itself to me.

Little by little, I learned with the thrill of a primary school child what this world consisted of. Of a population whose members can think only for the group, never for themselves. Of a single bee who is selected by chance to be fed more royal jelly than the others and therefore become the queen, the sole fertile member of the colony. Of how the queen leaves the hive once, and once only, in her life, for a mating flight during which she is impregnated enough to carry the genetic ability to produce over two million eggs in her lifetime, more than 2,000 in a single day. Of a feminist sorority where the men are kicked out as non-contributors, and even killed, before the winter sets in. Of a world where most communication and decision-making is done in the dark by smell and by pheromones. Of strange dances and heroic deaths. Of a creature who has worked alongside man for over 5,000 years, providing him with honey and being fed sugar in return over the long winter. Of a worker who labours so hard in the long summer days that she lives only a handful of weeks, in contrast to the three or four years of the queen, and who often dies in flight as her own wings shred with the efforts of her day-long foraging. And how all that the world has to show for her tiny life is a twelfth of a teaspoon of honey, and how that pot of honey would cost about £200,000 if all the bees that made it were paid the minimum wage. And above all, I learned that the honeybee population was in sharp decline, laid low by the effects of intensive farming, urbanisation, global warming and pesticides, and what this could eventually do to the human family on earth if allowed to run unchecked. Every line I read taught me something that, even as a boy brought up in the countryside, I had never known. Each sentence drew out of me the childlike fascination of a new and utterly compelling thing in my life. And I knew with certainty that I had to be part of it.

There are maybe 80 million domesticated hives in the world, and tonight I would be adding to their number by one.

Or not.

As darkness fell, I went out to check on the progress of my new guests, daring to believe as I did so that they had made the trip up the Egyptian cotton sheet into their new hive and were even now relaxing after an à la carte dinner and setting out a foraging strategy for the next day.

But it was not to be. In the rain and the damp, they had just stayed where they were, with only the boldest scouts troubling to check out what I had prepared for them. A dead bee is diminished in size, and at least half of my swarm had turned in on themselves and wouldn't be going anywhere, now or in the future. Bees can only ingest enough food to see them through a day or two, and the swarm that I had come across was apparently one that had already been out of the hive for enough time to take them close to the limit. Panicking, I removed the lid and crown board of the hive, and tipped the rest of the contents of the box, and the white sheet, into it. Maybe that would fix it.

An hour later I learned that it hadn't, when I went up with my torch to see whether there had been an improvement to the situation. Where all those years ago Mr Fowler's hive had been a seething mass of busy life when we had opened it, mine had the quiet air of death. Preferring to leave the lid closed so that I didn't disturb them yet again, I put my ear to the thin, metal-plated roof, and heard only silence.

For a while I just stood there in the rain and wondered what I had done, and how much better the colony would have been if I had left them entirely alone.

An email from Jim later that evening asked how I had got on, and I couldn't bring myself to answer it. I just decided to clean out the hive once it was daylight, and dry, and take a solemn oath not to touch another bee until I had learned how to keep them alive. Or avoid them for ever.

Months later, I came to realise that this five-minute period was another of the *Sliding Doors* moments of my life, only minus the sliding doors, the train or Gwyneth Paltrow. If events had not organised themselves as they did the following spring, the incident would have just been another enthusiasm in a life spent carelessly harvesting and discarding them. If the metaphorical doors had closed on this episode, I would have forgotten all about it, and it would have joined parascending, rock climbing and a host of other unlikely pastimes in the 'didn't quite come off' list. The old hive would have rotted slowly away unseen by the compost heap, a monument to an untutored enthusiasm, and that would have been that.

As it was, the doors hung tantalisingly open throughout the coming winter.

Chapter 2

THE BEARD

The following March

....

*Start where you are. Use what
you have. Do what you can.*
ARTHUR ASHE

....

The first thing I noticed was the beard. We don't get many of them round here.

The face behind it was talking to Caroline at the village pub, where we had dropped in after a long walk with the dogs.

'This is Duncan and Luzaan,' she said. 'They've just moved into the village. Duncan wants to play cricket and doesn't know who to talk to, so I said "you".'

That was a fair one. I help to run a social team, one that is always fated to be on the lookout for new players, so the arrival of a younger, robust-looking man into the neighbourhood boded well for the coming season. However, it also turned out that Duncan ran a small fruit and vegetable business out of New Covent Garden in London, and his opportunities to play would be dictated by the night-time market hours he worked. Apparently cabbages and courgettes prefer to operate in the hours of darkness, and so there was no prospect of these being amended to suit his cricketing commitments.

'I'll come whenever I can,' he told me. 'It's amazing how little sleep you need when there's something good going on.'

On our way out of the pub, Duncan noticed a little set of shelves where local produce – jam, chocolates, pickles and the like – was sold. He picked up a small pot of honey.

'Blimey!' he said. 'Seven pounds for that? I'm in the wrong business.'

It was indeed expensive, but we all gathered around the pot and admitted that it was beautiful, its dark clarity enhanced by the light streaming through the pub window, and its simple hand-written label announced that it had come from a garden not two hundred yards away. Its presence in my hand stirred a faint memory in me that was nearly a year old.

I explained about my disaster a year ago, and the continued existence of the mausoleum hive at the top end of my garden.

'I've always fancied keeping bees,' Duncan said. He saw it very much as one of the dividends of moving into a small village with his young family.

'You can have the hive with my compliments,' I told him. Jim had told me in no uncertain terms that he didn't want to see it back. 'I don't think it's my sort of thing.'

'You should try it again. You just need a bee-buddy. I'm sort of serious. Let me know if you want to give it another go, and I'll go halves.'

'Halves?' I asked him.

'Yup. Halves. Cost, work, honey. Sink or swim.'

'Why not have it at yours?' I didn't even know where he lived, but it seemed worth asking the question.

'Bees and small children don't mix.' In the months to come, we would prove many times over that bees and big children don't mix, either.

I walked back up the road with Caroline, and told her that, far from reopening an old wound as I had feared when he started talking about honey, he had reignited some small pilot light of interest in my system, the bit that told me that I wasn't done with this hobby yet. And that if people like us didn't get on with it, then the bees would go on declining and the whole country would be on a diet of lentils, Quorn and Channel 4 documentaries. While she didn't exactly want to join in herself, she seemed keen enough that we gave it a go. She was way ahead of me on her environmental journey at the time and, as an artist, had the instinctive and positive feel for things that would benefit the soul as opposed to the wallet.

'After all, we live in the right place,' she said, and it was hard to argue. We had been lucky enough to buy our cottage in the early 1990s before prices went mad. Now even the tiniest cottages round here sell for a king's ransom. Our house and one and a half acres of land lay on the edge of an upland village above the valley of the River Rother, and we were surrounded to the west, north and east by a field, a wood and a National Trust deer park respectively. Not a day went by when we didn't feel blessed to be there, when we didn't dig our bare toes into the dewy grass and feel nature rising up through us. It was the nest in which we had raised our two boys, and equally the nest from which, when fully fledged, they had flown in the previous year or two. During our time here we had tried our luck with sheep, cows, horses and even chickens to various degrees of success, from not very much to none at all, so what could be so difficult about a small wooden hive of bees tucked away out of sight? At the very worst, it would just be 'one of those things'.

Later in the evening, I sent Duncan a text:

'Good to meet. Nets are next Weds evening near Winchester. Can give you a lift over. And did you really mean what you said about bees? R'

A metallic 'ping' on my phone at 3.00am announced that Duncan was catching up with personal correspondence after presumably processing a bulk order of salad crops for the kitchen of some big City law firm.

'Yup', it said. For a few months, this was the longest text he ever managed to send me. Most of them consisted of either two exclamation marks or some emoji he had found on his phone.

From now on, with only an owl as its friend, the phone would have to stay downstairs at night, and on 'mute'.

Seasons wait for no man, and when we met up the following Friday evening, we were immediately faced with our first dilemma.

On the one hand, we knew that the proficient beekeeper has all their preparation for the coming season done and dusted by the end of February: the equipment maintenance, the Varroa mite control, the checking of food sources and the colony build-up have all been done, and the beekeeper is lying back on their sofa listening to old Cat Stevens CDs and waiting for it all to be delivered by their little friends. By these standards, we were hopelessly late already. On the other hand, we were fairly typical of our sex, and we wanted the instant gratification of honey coming out of our ears by the approaching autumn, which meant acting quickly and decisively now. So we started with that most decisive and English of activities, buying ourselves a notebook. In hindsight, we probably spent more time choosing that little notebook than any other bit of kit we bought.

We sat round our kitchen table the next morning, delighted with our purchase, on the cover of which Duncan started drawing a cartoon bee, together with an annoying pun on the word 'bee'.

'It needs an index,' I suggested. 'Every book has to have an index.'

So on the first page, Duncan wrote a formal 'Upperfold Bee Farm' in block capitals, and on each of the next twelve double pages he added the months of the year, starting with March. Calling it by the name 'farm' dignified it with a certain formality that, we hoped, might instil in the pair of us a work ethic appropriate to the task in hand.

'It needs a cash section, so we can see how much profit we're making as we go along,' I added, so Duncan laid out a basic income and expenditure form in some of the middle pages.

Had we known then what we came to know over the next few months, we might have thought more discriminatingly about the use of the word 'profit' at the head of the page: 'profit' was a word that we were unlikely to see before the reunification of the Korean peninsula. Then we added some pages for 'inspection register', and finally left a few pages blank at the back for the unexpected. The little notebook was so beautifully laid out that it was almost tempting to stop there. I laid it on the kitchen table by the fruit bowl, more to register a sense of progress than for any useful reason. Its presence there was a signal to the outside world that we were in business.

A quick trip to the north end of the garden to inspect the

mausoleum hive ended with the inevitable conclusion that, if we were to be at the top of our game from the word 'go', we needed to invest in a new one. Although we started with eBay, we very quickly persuaded ourselves that you got what you paid for in life, and that our first major investment should be an eye-wateringly expensive, beautiful, new and complete National Cedar Hive from our local bee equipment wholesaler, Paynes. Little did we know at the time, but it was the beginning of a commercial relationship that has almost led Paynes to a billion-dollar listing on Nasdaq.

'That's 325 quid,' I moaned. 'We were going to try to spend £250 on everything, hive included.'

'A mere detail at this stage,' Duncan assured me, putting on the kettle. 'They didn't build the Channel Tunnel by being on budget.'

We knew that the local association had a beekeeping auction coming up in three weeks at a nearby agricultural college, and figured we could get everything else we needed from there, second hand, and accompanied no doubt by the copious advice of further bearded people, almost certainly called Seth or Jethro.

'Books!' said Duncan. 'We need to get ourselves a couple of teach-yourself books.'

And so we went on to Amazon and spent a further £36 on four separate books, on the basis that we could each read two at a time, books that ranged from the entirely dry and technical *Haynes Bee Manual* to a viciously feminist pamphlet that seemed to be suggesting that, as with humans, the only good drone was a dead one.

All this preparation was thirsty work, and we congratulated ourselves on the immense progress we had made during the morning over a beer.

'We're basically there,' I said to Duncan. 'Once we have bought suits and tools at the auction, what more could we possibly need?'

'Bees?' asked Caroline innocently, as she walked past to get something out of the fridge.

Duncan and I looked at each other. She had a point, even if we hadn't asked her opinion.

At the start of a season, the average bee colony is a testament to the sheer survival instinct in nature.

From a high point in the previous summer of maybe 50,000 bees, the hive will have reduced to about a tenth of that, and they will have spent the coldest part of the winter huddled together around the queen for warmth, shivering their wing muscles to create heat, and taking it in turns to be on the outside like penguins on an Antarctic ice floe. On warmer days, the whole huddle will move to a different part of the hive where fresh honey is stored, which is why a protracted cold spell can kill them off: they starve to death through their inability to move, rather than by freezing.

As heat slowly returns to their world, and the days start to get longer, the queen resumes laying eggs and the workers begin to head back out of the hive to forage for the nectar that will become this season's honey. Plants like snowdrops, crocus and hellebore will provide enough temptation in nectar and pollen for them to fly as early as the end of January, even though the hive they fly from is still in full winter routine. Soon enough, the population of the hive begins to accelerate towards its maximum level by about July and August.

So what Duncan and I needed to achieve from a start point in the middle of March was to find a ready-made colony, and place it into our expensive new hive in the hope that it would meet with their collective approval and they would get on with things without too much interference from us. Strong and well-behaved colonies – that's the yellow brick road for people like us. The colony's behaviour tends to take its lead from the queen, and from her own parentage, so it is essential, particularly for the rookie beekeeper, to buy her from a trusted, well-reviewed source.

Another simple internet search took us around any number of suppliers of nucleus colonies or 'nucs' – the ready-made colony in miniature that the novice beekeeper needs to get going. By degrees, we narrowed this down to two or three that we liked the look of, and finally went for a farmer in the middle of Oxfordshire because he looked friendly and was reasonable value. We duly ordered a six-frame 'Spring Nuc', complete with box, brood, bees, a bit of honey and a new marked queen. After all, when you are inspecting the hive later in the summer, looking through 50,000 bees for one that is a bit bigger than the rest but is otherwise pretty identical, it helps if she has a bit of colour daubed on the back of her thorax. To the two vital questions, 'When can we have her?' and 'How much do you want from us?', the thick Ukrainian accent came back over the phone line with the replies, 'mid of April' and '£150'. Which produced in turn the twin confirmation that we would be apiarists within the month, and that we had so far spent £521 out of our original budget of £250, all of which was solemnly entered into our little bee notebook. We decided to ignore the cost of the petrol, in case it started to depress us. As the Greeks have occasionally worked out for themselves, you can take fiscal responsibility too far if you are not careful.

Assuming everything we did from now on was perfect, and everything went as right as it possibly could, we would get our first honey in September. And as we all know, you can rely on nature never to produce surprises.

A few days later, the hive arrived on the doorstep in kit form.

My first instinct as I unpacked it was that our £325 had been well spent, very much driven by the impression of there being a great number of exciting-looking bits in the package, and that each bit must have cost something to make. My second thought, namely that we could have this assembled and out in its new plot by nightfall, was rudely shot down by Duncan, who dropped in during the evening on his way to work in New Covent Garden.

'It's bare wood,' he said, 'and it needs painting.' He fingered the cedar planks for a while, then added: 'Every single outside surface. Otherwise, it will just rot and we'll have to buy another.'

It was an early discovery of an essential difference between the two of us. Whereas I would find a short cut to an existing short cut if it got the job done quicker, Duncan's way was to go through as many stages of preparation as possible in any given job, and then add a few more. He didn't just mean paint the hive; he meant clean, sand, prime, undercoat and then topcoat it, which looked to me suspiciously like five different jobs, and that was before we even tried to assemble it. Given that the hive was at my house, because his was full of children and fruit boxes, it didn't take a genius to work out who might be doing the lion's share of the painting. Perfectionist Pedant was working with Attention Deficit Man, which could either turn out to be an ideal mix of creative tension or a recipe for disaster.

The type of hive we had chosen was a National, a derivative of one patented by an American pastor called Lorenzo Lorraine Langstroth in the mid-nineteenth century. He was trying to come up with a formula that allowed the honey to be taken, and the bees to be regularly inspected, without the whole thing falling to pieces. Essentially, it consists of two boxes: a big one below called the 'brood box', where the eggs are laid and the brood raised; and one or more smaller ones above called 'supers', where the beekeeper entices his workers to make pure honey. Each box has a series of eleven vertically hanging wax-filled frames. The boxes are separated by a grille called a queen excluder, which all the bees except the queen can pass through, which means that the supers above contain pure honey, and not a mix of honey and brood. Holding it all up is a stand and a mesh floor, and above it there is a crown board and a lid, which combine to provide ventilation throughout the year.

Enthusiasts can, and do, go on for days, weeks in fact, about the advantages of one type of hive over another, but novices like Duncan and me tend to go for the Nationals as they are easy to assemble, simple to transport and, most important, interchangeable with fellow beekeepers. They aren't as attractive as the WBC hives (the pretty ones with the pointy roofs that most people associate with the craft), but they get the job done.

So, for the next few evenings, I laid out all the wooden component parts on my garage floor and started preparing them for action, the trick being to use primer and undercoat when Duncan was looking, and topcoat only when he wasn't. The less he popped by, the quicker it went, and the quicker it went, the more suspicious he became; however, by the weekend it was ready for assembly, and all that was left to do before next month's auction, and the arrival of our nuc, was to select a site.

～❦

Out in the wild, bees aren't that fussy about where they live. They like to find something like the inside of a hollowed-out tree and set up shop in the dark, sheltered space that this provides. What constitutes a suitable home for them is hard-wired into the scout bees' instincts, and is generally uncomplicated.

But throw a beekeeper in the mix, and you suddenly find a whole list of complex ingredients for the desirable siting of your hive. Briefly, these are: easy access, good drainage, a nearby water source, dappled sunlight and protection from the wind. Ideally, there should be some sort of shelter behind the hive, and it should face more east than west (to get them going earlier with the morning sun) and more north than south (to keep them out of the prevailing south-west wind). Caroline had quite strong views about not having 50,000 bees in the immediate garden, so we duly relegated ourselves to a far corner of the paddock where we kept a few Southdown sheep, and staked out a suitable spot in the lee of a damson tree.

I looked up at the white damson blossom as Duncan and I were clearing the undergrowth below, and saw with a frisson of excitement a couple of honeybees hovering from flower to flower in the flat spring sunlight. Bees forage for distances of up to three miles from their hive, depending on what food sources are available, and in what quantity, so these might have been wild, or they might have come from another domestic colony in the vicinity. But what thrilled the very children in our souls was that they would shortly be joined by a thriving colony that would be our own. Britain has lost a third of its honeybees and a quarter of its bumble-bee species since the turn of the century, and this spot, and this moment, was to be the start of our own tiny contribution to reversing the trend.

On the face of it, the home we were offering them was idyllic. If you were a bee, then this would be St George's Hill or Sandbanks, with stratospheric house prices and excellent schools in the area to match. We were privileged to live on the edge of a tiny village which was, itself, on the edge of a park, full to the brim with trees and vegetation more or less untouched by chemicals or pesticides. Just to our north was the village common and, beyond that, two or three hundred acres of beech woods sloping down into the Weald, all red-hot areas for our bees to go and forage once they were in residence. Downhill to our south was the bigger village we were part of, the Rother valley below that, and the whale-back spine of the 100-mile South Downs ridge beyond. No day passed by on my commute to and from work when I didn't thank the god of undeserved benefits that we had fetched up here a quarter of a century before. Doing so had enabled us to throw ourselves energetically at our plot of land, and to marinade our children's minds in the slow-moving rhythms of the natural year.

As far as bees are concerned, you only need to look around to work out what they are going to feed on. Hedgerows and woods are seasonal providers of mixed blossom, farmers tend to rotate crops in their fields, and gardens can and should have a mix of flowers that will provide interest for bees for the nine months of the year that isn't deepest winter. Cities and towns are fine, as they have parks, gardens and other open spaces all around. So it's only if you are surrounded by, say, a nuclear reprocessing plant, a sewage works and an open-cast strip mine on three sides of your property that you might reach the conclusion that beekeeping isn't quite the hobby for you. In other words, most people live in the right place to keep a hive or two.

The more we read, the more we knew that our contribution to reversing the plight of the bee was desperately needed. They are up against almost everything in today's environment. Nothing so informed and galvanised our efforts at the beginning as the predicament of beneficial insect species in the world in which we raised our children. Intensive farming, monoculture, habitat loss, urban development, climate change, pesticides, disease, and invasive species all come together in a poisonous cocktail for the humble bee, bumble or otherwise. Go on any bee association's blog and you will find far more about different Varroa treatments and the dangers of the Asian hornet than you ever will about maximising honey crops. Because beekeepers are on the front line. The problem, as with global warming and deforestation to name two equivalents, is that the fate of the pollinating bee never quite makes a significant enough shadow on the radar of immediate problems in an average life – the mortgage, the rat race and the weekly shopping bills – for a critical mass of us to do something about it. They never quite make it to the top section of mankind's to-do list. To achieve this they would have to replace the really important stuff like maximising shareholder returns and carpeting fields with new housing. But when they're gone, they're gone.

So, to establish an agreeable precedent, we set up a couple of deckchairs by the gleaming white hive that we had finished assembling, and toasted with cheap Spanish lager whatever the future of this adventure might bring. Any old fool can be uncomfortable, was the way we saw it, and even environmental activism needs its rewards.

'What do we actually do with them when we've got them?' asked Duncan. 'I mean, what actually *is* beekeeping?'

Neither of us had a clue.

People with degrees always know best.

When I mentioned Duncan's irritating question to Caroline over supper that night, she said it was highly unlikely that someone in the area didn't run beekeeping courses, and why didn't we both sign up for one? My emotional answer ('Because I left school 40 years ago') was topped by her rational one ('If you learn how to do this, you just might end up not killing all the bees like you did last time'), and I couldn't argue with her. Not with any hope of coming out on top, anyway. After all, the South Downs Beekeeping Association was only a handful of miles away and was one of the most active in the land, always on the look-out for new converts to the cause.

'Teach a man to fish, and all that,' she said. 'That's what you're always telling the boys.'

Not for the last time in the process, my enthusiasm and impatience were running way ahead of the accompanying realities. In my mind's eye, I could already see the ranks of honey up on my larder shelf, could already hear the honest gratitude of departing visitors into whose outstretched hands I would be pressing jars of the stuff as miniature gifts.

I had started to keep a detailed diary, not just of the bee-keeping but also of the adventure around it. Into it I found myself bundling little bits of bee lore that I discovered during my researches, and a glossary of the new language that I was having to learn.

'It's lovely,' said Caroline when I showed it to her one evening. 'It looks like you're writing a book.'

'Absolutely not! How on earth could you jump to that conclusion?'

'I'm not sure. It must be something to do with the fact that you've written "Chapter One" at the beginning.'

This had been entirely subconscious, but, in a way, she was right – it was that most hackneyed of things, a new chapter. I had reached that stage of life where each new development carried a deeper, and more urgent, significance. My children might have left home, but they hadn't taken my sense of parenthood with them, for a start, or the need to be needed. While they were growing up, I could point to their development as little achievements that were my own; once they were gone, so was that deception. Writing things down had always been how I dealt with such change. Or with anything else, for that matter.

What I was starting to write about in my little notebook, without fully knowing it, was the next bit of my life.

Keeping bees is about learning to work with nature. Most of what you need to know you pick up as you go along, learning by experience and by swapping thoughts with other enthusiasts, but there are some absolute basics that you need to grasp before you get going. You must understand the life cycle of the queen, the workers and the drones; you must know how to handle bees, learn how and why a swarm happens, and be able to identify the signs of disease. Everything else is for another day.

I am not proud to say that I lasted just one lesson.

I arrived for my first session the following Thursday evening in a serene woodland setting that could have come straight out of a 1930s rural novel. A small lean-to sheltered the bee suits that we would wear for our lesson, and everywhere in the still evening was the amplified sound of woodland birds defending their territories. Polite refugees from Middle England, for the next 90 minutes or so we sat on a couple of benches and listened to our instructor outlining the seriousness of what we were embarking on, and the responsibilities that this entailed. At no point in the introductory talk did he welcome us into his magical world; rather he told us that we were privileged to be there, and not to leave at the end of the session thinking we were beekeepers.

'Not quite what I was expecting,' whispered my neighbour as she pulled the veil over her head after he had finished. 'I thought this was supposed to be fun.'

Then I stood with the others over an open hive under the beech trees, smelling the smoke rising up as if it was the days of the old charcoal burners, and, for the first time I was shown how to handle bees. I noted other students, full of watchful humility, taking frames out of the brood box, like I had done, and looking with wonder at the life and work within.

It was an idyllic spot in which to dive deep into the world of bees for the very first time, an exercise that felt much like my first driving lesson out on the open road 40 years before, with all the sense of a rite of passage that this implied. We took it in turns to pull out the vertical frames and inspect first one side and then the other, for the whereabouts of the queen and any signs of future misbehaviour. The instructor had suggested that we all started as he would like us to go on, with ungloved hands, so that we would be less clumsy and grow to feel the mood of the bees; to my shame, I was in the half of the group that ignored him. He also carried a clipboard onto which, rather unnervingly, he wrote comments about us as we each took our turn. I dreaded to think what he was saying about me. 'Lacks courage', possibly, or 'handles bees like a herd of rhinoceroses'.

That Thursday evening out in the dapple-lit woods of the West Sussex Weald was enough to convince me that I had to teach myself. It wasn't that they weren't nice people, as they manifestly were; it wasn't that what they were saying and doing was boring, because it wasn't; it wasn't even that I was so arrogant that I thought I knew better than them from Day One. Far from it, I was genuinely terrified of my own incompetence. It was because they made it abundantly clear from the first minute that this was a slow process, and you had to complete the beginners' classes before they would accept you as an intermediate, and you had to complete the intermediate before they would allow you to become an expert and only then would they even think of supporting you as a beekeeper. Given that this support entailed other experts coming along and troubleshooting for you, and swarms being sent in your general direction by the association when they became available, it was worth having. The way Duncan and I saw our season, we would be unveiling pots of honey within six months; the way the teacher saw things, we would be lucky if we owned a hive by Lammas Eve in two years' time.

As Aristotle liked to say: 'The roots of education are bitter, but the fruit is sweet.' The great thing about having a New Covent Garden wholesaler on the books was that you could theoretically have the fruit straight away without bothering with the roots; and, not without a small shard of regret, I never went back again.

Into the expenditure register that night went another £20, the cost of the classes I had booked into, bringing the running total up to £541.

We were going to need a bloody good crop of honey.

'This bee business,' said Caroline as we got ready for bed that evening. 'Are you going to take it seriously?'

I could tell that she was nervous at the speed with which I had abandoned the formal education, and the slightly intemperate language that I may have used to describe the instructor.

'Of course. Why do you ask?'

It was a stupid question. I knew exactly why she had asked. I started brushing my teeth to avoid a complicated discussion – solid marriages, after all, being based on a fine instinct as to when is not a good time to talk about something.

'It's just that I think you could be really good at it if you took a bit of trouble and learned the basics. And if you got really good at it, I think you would enjoy it far more than if you didn't. Instead of clearing dead bees out of a rotten old hive, you could be selling your own honey, and becoming an expert. And Duncan looks like the kind of person who wants to learn alongside you.' She paused, gauging whether she still had my attention. 'It's an opportunity for you. At least think about it.'

By Caroline's standards, this was a lengthy speech, and I knew where it had come from. She had seen my various enthusiasms wax and wane alongside the moon over the years, their expensive detritus used for a season and then piled up in our attic on the spurious notion that they could be sold on eBay one of these days. I lay in bed for a while and realised that this one had to be different from the others because it involved living creatures, even though I was still some months from knowing how emotionally committed I would become. A little owl yeeked from its nightly staging post on the branch of the tulip tree outside our bedroom and I rolled over.

'I promise,' I said, eventually.

But she was fast asleep.

Chapter 3

THE AUCTION

April

....

We are not the sum of our possessions.
GEORGE H.W. BUSH

....

It starts young, and we can't help ourselves.

As males, we need the toys that go with what we do. When I was a child, my first bike was quite a plain thing, but once I had added a horn, a bell, mudguards, a speedometer and a load of stickers, it looked less like a form of transport and more like a Tibetan prayer wheel. On its own, the bike was impersonal, but covered with the detritus of my visits to the local bike shop after birthdays and Christmas, it was undeniably mine. I'm not entirely sure what statement it made about me, but it made one nonetheless.

Duncan and I had set ourselves two financial targets for Upperfold Bee Farm: first, that we would outlay no more than £250 on our new hobby, and secondly, that we would break even in our second year of production. I am not clear which hallucinogenic drugs we were tucking into when we made that decision, and when we invented that threshold, but it's hard to argue that something so crass could have been the product of genetics alone. Even to non-accounting brains like ours, the maths were straightforward: if you could clear £5 for a small pot of honey and you had £250 of directly attributable costs, then you had to produce and sell 50 pots in the course of the year to break even. However, our capital outlay for this year was already £541 and rising rapidly, which pointed to the need for over 100 pots, and then only if we didn't spend another penny on equipment. Whatever else happened, the paint, the petrol, the nuts, bolts, screws, feeders, sugar syrup and disinfectant would all have to be put down to 'general housekeeping' while no one was looking.

The statistics behind all this were not, on the face of it, encouraging. One jar of honey is the result of the combined efforts of over 20,000 bees over a period of time, and they will cumulatively fly 50,000 miles and visit two million flowers in order to produce it. A British beehive averages out at 24 pounds of honey in a quiet year, and maybe up to 35 or 40 in a long, warm summer. Throw all of that together with our financial targets, and we either needed to get ten hives going with no further financial outlay, or manage the most productive bees in the western hemisphere. Or we were going to have to charge about £40 a pot which, even in the Home Counties, might be asking just a bit too much.

And yet, and yet. We still wanted to be magnificent bee-keepers, always one step ahead of the others and admired by the people who passed the field and saw us working in it; we wanted new equipment, and not just someone's cast-offs from eBay. We hadn't yet even gone to the auction and acquired spare frames and foundation, let alone the tools, smokers and other stuff that we would need along the way. And if you stole their honey at the end of the summer, it was going to be down to you to feed the bees yourself, or they would starve. It looked very much as though if you wanted to make a small fortune from beekeeping, you needed to start with a large one.

'What about the beers?' asked Caroline innocently. 'Do they count as expenditure as well?'

In our brave new world, beers were a metaphor for progress.

Each time we achieved something of significance – and we came to realise over the months that we could set the bar for 'significance' wherever we liked – we would uncap a beer to ensure that we had marked the event both appropriately and respectfully. This, by the way, is just one of the male's unsung contributions to human endeavour.

Beers, or coffee if it was that time of day, also allowed Duncan and me to get to know each other better in those early weeks, in that magical phase of a new friendship where each revelation is a surprise and each avenue of conversation an invitation for discovery. Despite the fact that we were at different phases of our lives by about 25 years, the intersection of the Venn Diagram between us was a wide one, particularly when it came to a sense of the ridiculous, a love of a shared adventure, and appreciation of the natural history around us. Our straddling of the various roles ensured that one of us (him) was the disciplined, practical and reliable strength in the partnership, and one of us (me) was the more challenging, dynamic and assertive one. Expressed as weaknesses, this meant that Duncan took bloody ages to get anything done, while I specialised in spending hours pissing people off by dreaming up things we would never do anyway. Vitally, though, we both knew how to be part of a team.

Wisdom also taught me that I needed this diversion more than he did, although it would be the best part of a year before I understood why.

The basic equipment needed to make honey is, well, a bee.

Bees in the wild will site their colonies in any suitable cavity and just get on with it. The comb is natural and simply fills up the available space. Provided they protect it from predators like wasps and mice, they get to gorge on it through the cold months of winter. This process is entirely free, and they have been doing it since they evolved into their current shape and form 30 million years ago. The problem that this presents us, and other thieving mammals, is that in order to access the honey, you need almost by definition to destroy the nest. Clearly, this is not an entirely sustainable business model.

In domesticating the bee, and needing to have practical access to the honey within the hive, it is humans who have complicated things and provided the scary shopping list with which we were now confronted. For thousands of years, bees were housed in skeps – basically just an upturned basket – but skeps are a particularly inflexible way of keeping them, with no easy way of removing the honey, and even less of inspecting them regularly. So the moveable-frame hive was developed in the mid-1800s, and it has been evolving ever since.

The equipment that you buy is primarily supposed to make your life easier, and to maximise the chance of hosting a healthy colony. By having the correct kit for the job, and a routine that dovetailed with the natural rhythms of the bees, we were making things as easy as they theoretically could be, so that we didn't end up losing swarms and encouraging predation, or hosting a virus. More importantly, it gave Duncan the opportunity to send me hundreds of pointless kit-related emails in the wee small hours of the night, and for the staff at Paynes to order a few more travel brochures for the Maldives.

A layman's guide to what the modern amateur beekeeper needs, on top of the hive itself, might run something like this.

Protective clothing. A heavy cotton canvas top with attached veil is all you need. The key is to make sure that there are no holes in it, especially the veil, as a disturbed worker is certain to find it. Goatskin or latex protective gloves are essential add-ons, as the heroics quickly stop once you start getting regularly stung on your fingers. Beekeeping is not supposed to be a branch of masochism. Below the belt, it is just a question of serviceable and robust trousers, tucked into socks. And of avoiding the mistake of fully protecting your top half and then forgetting to swap your shorts for trousers in your enthusiasm to get among your bees. Flip-flops disappoint, too, in this regard. Price range £10–£120.

A hive tool. This comes in many forms and costs no more than £5, unless you are Duncan and me, in which case it costs about £20. Bees make an awful lot of propolis, wax and honey, all of which sticks surfaces together when you are trying to work with them, and they often need prizing apart. The classic hive tool has a thin wedge at one end and a J-hook at the other, and is also handy for opening beer bottles, if carefully selected. £5–£20.

A smoker. The general thinking is that smoke calms bees down because the incoming fumes make them instinctively think there is a forest fire nearby, and that they need to gorge themselves for a long flight to safety in consequence. If this is true, our bees must be beginning to wonder why there is a forest fire locally at 11.00 sharp every Saturday morning, immediately followed by someone taking their roof off and pulling all the furniture around. The key function of a smoker is to be almost impossible to light, and to extinguish itself just at the time you really need it. £20–£40.

Spare foundation. These are the wax sheets that fill the frames, and which the bees subsequently draw out, and make honey in. Some have thin wire threaded through, which makes them stronger when they are carrying the weight of honey and brood, while others are plain. Putting new frames together is, theoretically, a lovely occupation for a long winter's evening, but not if you have the manual dexterity of an Emperor penguin. £8 for a pack of ten sheets.

Queen catcher. Vital piece of simple equipment for isolating the queen from the rest of the colony for marking, or some other reason. So vital, in fact, that four years have gone by and we still haven't bought one. Or if we did, we lost it. Or didn't know how to use it. £5–£10.

Feeders. One way or another, the bees will need to be fed over the long winter months, and unfortunately it's not as simple as putting a packet of Cheesy Wotsits in the hive every couple of days. They will either want sugar syrup or some form of soft fondant, both of which need a suitable method of delivery. Over the years, we have chosen the fondant route, partly because it is rather less complicated to install in the hive. £5 to £30, depending on whether you go for the plastic bowl or the wooden tray.

Treatments, screens and nuc boxes. Stuff by and large for later in the season, and which we will get on to.

Spinner. Also called extractor. The bees produce honey in a frame, which needs to be uncapped (the wax cut away) and then centrifugally spun, drained and filtered. As with combine harvesters for bigger farmers, the spinner is a relatively complex and expensive piece of kit and normally something that can be passed around from apiary to apiary rather than everyone buying one. Or so everyone thinks. Theoretically, it's a good idea; practically, as with joint ownership of a combine harvester, most people in the area tend to take honey off their bees at roughly the same time. From £100 to £500, but readily available second-hand for less.

Jars. Lots of them, although possibly not in Year 1. And, yes, your kitchen cupboards may well be stuffed to the brim with useable old Hellmann's mayonnaise bottles and peanut butter jars, but this rag, tag and bobtail approach is not necessarily designed to dignify the efforts of your bees. Duncan, whose first resort was to outlay cash on any given situation, was strangely tight-fisted when it came to jars. From 30p to £1 each.

In our preparation for the coming auction, we also added 'spare hive' to this list, because you never know when someone is going to call you up and say that they have found a swarm in their garden, and would you like it. If you have an empty hive with frames and foundation in place, then all you need to do in theory is take the swarm and dump it in. Swarms are still the cheapest way of becoming a bigger beekeeper, and we therefore set ourselves a limit of £40 to acquire an old National hive. Very quickly, you come to realise that you should never be too proud to accept someone else's cast-offs, or too mean to furnish other people with your own.

Just as there are certain people who should never be brain surgeons, so there are people who should under no circumstances be allowed to attend an auction. And the immediate problem for the Upperfold Bee Farm was that both Duncan and I belonged firmly in this category. The person you need to send to an auction is an expert in the field with the self-control of a Trappist monk, not two ignorant and over-enthusiastic novices.

The evening before the auction we studied the lotting list carefully so that we could be as organised as our level of knowledge allowed, and would know not only what lots to bid on, but what was the highest we could go to. The way we looked at it all, we might not be experts, but we could be well prepared. I had emailed Jim, in his capacity as a half-way house of knowledge between complete ignorance and the didactic lecturing of the hardened pro, and asked him what he thought we needed kit-wise to get ourselves on the road.

'Your brain examining,' he had replied. 'Plus some anti-histamine and some note cards.'

'Note cards?'

'For apologising to your neighbours when your bees sting them and crap on their nice white sheets.'

The list ran to over 300 lots, and included a rather disappointingly low percentage of things that we knew about, and a correspondingly high one of things about which we had no idea at all. Anything that you could think of in the world of bee husbandry, and quite a lot you couldn't, was going to be available: from crown boards to Varroa mesh, via Langstroth supers, honey buckets, pollen traps, skeps and even a pack of bee tobacco. At the top end of the value chain were complete hives of inspected bees, and propping it all up far below was a second-hand paperback book on their sex lives.

'It would be good to know what they get up to when the lights are out,' said Duncan with enthusiasm, and ticked it off with a red pen that meant we were to be active bidders. By the time we were ready, we had produced a list of the lots we really needed, lots that would be good to have, plus the ones that we would only bid on if there was little interest and we could get them cheap:

List A: Essential
Two bee suits
Two pairs of protective gloves

One smoker

Two hive tools

List B: Discretionary

Second-hand National hive

Spare foundation

Top feeder

Books on bees, especially sex

List C: Under no circumstances, unless absolutely given away

Spinner

More bees

Other stuff, unless about sex, in which case possibly

As with the buyer who acquired Van Gogh's 'Sunflowers' for $40 million at Christie's back in 1987, so with us: we put a price range against each lot we were going to bid for, and a figure above which we should never go. That way we would apply the disciplines necessary not to be financially cleaned out once we were there.

Before parting for the evening, we established two further rules, to the effect that we would bring £200 cash only, so that we could limit the damage, and would not bid before Lot 30, by which time we would have more of an idea of the process and the anticipated values.

For a time after our arrival at Brinsbury Agricultural College the following morning, everything went to plan.

We parked the car in the right place, registered and paid our £5 entry fee, then walked unobtrusively up and down the lots, which had been laid out in long lines on a large area of hardstanding. The idea was to look like practised apiarists, not like no-hopers who didn't actually own any bees yet and whose only honey was in a Tesco jar on the breakfast table.

Anyone who was anyone in the world of West Sussex bees was there. There were grizzled old men with heavy beards and whipcord trousers held up by bailer twine; there were assertive women with clipboards and polystyrene cups of institutional coffee, giving instructions; there was a teenage boy in broken glasses and a West Ham strip who seemed to know more about the subject than anyone else. There were Jack Russells tugging at leads to sniff at the back ends of other Jack Russells, bored children who had been dragged along, and ordinary people from all over the region who just enjoyed the togetherness of a shared interest. Some were standing proudly by their own lots, waiting to explain them to potential purchasers; others were walking with deliberation from lot to lot, making knowledgeable notes on the sheets, and passing ruthlessly by when something failed to measure up. The passing talk was of Asian hornets, bakers' fondant and foundationless frames; of swarm control techniques, clearer boards and drone brood timing. All we could do was walk up and down, nodding sagely from time to time, then say something technical that might get overheard, like 'genetic diversity' or 'the efficacy of marjoram'. This wasn't just an auction; it was a central part of the architecture of the social life of the regional beekeeping community.

Gone are the times when the only people who kept bees were countrymen like Mr Fowler, with their small back gardens and their deep inherited knowledge. These days, there are about 250,000 working hives knocking around in the UK, in the hands of about 50,000 beekeepers, many fewer hives than there were, to be sure, but much more widely spread than before. Most of these are small-scale hobbyists like us (there are perhaps 50 proper farmers who do it as a business), and many of them keep bees in the heart of our cities. If you were to count the feral colonies and the unregistered ones, London probably supports 10,000 colonies itself, and has thriving beekeeping associations. Given that a worker will travel up to three miles to forage, you could put a hive almost anywhere, and, so long as you did the husbandry well, expect a decent crop of honey. Here around us were country folk like gamekeepers, gardeners and farmers, but also university lecturers, policemen and supermarket check-out staff – just as knowledgeable, and just as committed. The digital age has paradoxically made it all very much easier to learn one of humanity's oldest farming techniques. And it has rendered it classless and ageless to boot.

Beekeeping crosses borders too. High up on a Tuscan hillside that summer, I came across a tiny shop that sold nothing but the products of the Apicoltura Apililia syndicate. Jar after jar. Flavour after flavour. Eucalyptus, lemon, orange, melon, dandelion, sunflower, thorn, and others that I had never even heard of, to the centre of each crop of which a couple of hives would have been moved at the critical point the previous season. The shopkeeper spoke in a strong Italian dialect. Neither of us had a word in common. And yet he spent twenty minutes thrilling me in sign language with his secret world of Apennine beekeeping. And, at the end of it all, I thrilled him in return by paying 8 euros for the smallest pot of rosemary honey in the known world. A year later, having apparently learned nothing from my experience as an apiarist, I was chased away by a swarm of bees on a Greek hillside, having cheekily wandered into a field to see what they were up to. Like birdwatching, you can take the hobby of beekeeping anywhere.

'You got your paddle?' asked one of the stewards. The auction was about to start.

'Paddle?' I asked her.

'Yes. Paddle with your number on to bid with. You can't bid without it, my darling!'

So we retrieved our designated paddle from the organiser's desk, and, regarding the lady as a new friend, asked her to talk us through some of the lots we liked, and what we should bid for them.

'George wants them,' she said about a pair of brand-new protective jackets. 'But he won't ever pay more than

£30 each out of principle. And the Secretary is after a new smoker. Probably this one. I reckon £15 should get it for you.' Everyone not only knew everyone else, but also what they needed and how much they would be prepared to pay for it. The boy with the broken glasses had been shadowing us, and now sidled alongside to see what intelligence he could gather. The smoker was obviously going to be subject to a three-way tussle.

'Hello, Ryan,' said our friend. 'What are you after today?'

'Oh. Nothing, really. Just seeing what's around.' He had a catalogue that was marked up against almost every single lot, so the chances of him being interested in buying nothing were approximately zero. We felt that we had unwittingly homed in on the Godfather.

'Right! Let's get started then,' called out one of the grizzled men with whipcord trousers. 'I've just had me knee done, so I'll hand over to Brian once I run out of puff.' He was standing by behind Lot 1, and clearly the bidders were expected to stand the other side.

'Lot 1, then,' he said. 'Ten five-metre lengths of candle wick. Someone start me at three quid.'

No one did.

'It's going to be a long day if you're all like this,' he said. 'How about two quid, then?'

It was enough to prime the pump. Someone raised their paddle and then the price went up in 50 pence increments until I noticed that one of the three bidders still involved was Duncan.

I mouthed a silent scream of 'Why?' at him, but it was too late. An ominous pause in the bidding meant that Upperfold Bee Farm was now the proud possessor of Lot 1, 50 metres of candle wick, and about £8 of debt. At the current rate, and by bidding on things that we didn't even know existed, let alone needed, we would have blown our £200 in time to be home by lunch. For a man who spent half his working life bidding for brassicas in the febrile night-time atmosphere of a New Covent Garden trading floor, Duncan was redefining uselessness in the South Downs noontime.

We watched the next twenty or so lots from a distance, determined not to be the *ingénues* among the experts. Bidding was brisk and brief: the auctioneer only ever gave a few seconds after the last bid before bringing his fist down onto the clipboard in his other hand and saying 'Done!'

Lot 27 was the two bee suits. It turned out that while George didn't actually want them, plenty of others did, and they went for £85 to a vast tweed-clad lady who wouldn't have fitted into either of them. It seemed unfair both to us and to her, but it was way above the maximum we had agreed on. A couple more tatty suits went, and we missed both of them. Same with the best of the smokers, where we were taken out by a man with a passing resemblance to Brian Blessed. It was some compensation that we landed the bee sex book for

£1.50, and a box of 50 small jars for £12, which I fancied might be quite useful later in the summer.

'A man could get used to this auction lark,' said Duncan as he headed off to the makeshift café to buy a couple of bits of lemon drizzle cake to go with our flask of tea. 'Don't do anything stupid while I'm away.'

I didn't, but what I did do was come out top in the bidding for Lot 76, a mating hive that looked quite pretty, and as if it would be useful somewhere down the line.

'It was a steal at £23,' I told him when he returned, but he seemed unimpressed. He took charge again, and I watched him out of the corner of my eye, wondering briefly what on earth had brought him into this strange and brave new world. At the stage of life where he had more demands on his time than he had ever had before, or would ever have again, he had chosen to throw in his lot with a person he barely knew, and on a pastime that was still hidden in the mists of mythology. Subconsciously, though, I had known the answer all along: we do these things for days like this, and because we just do, and they don't discriminate over how suitable their presence in our lives might be when they first tap us on the shoulder. After all, any old species can just sit on its nest and stare at the soft furnishings, but humans aren't any old species.

Back down to earth at the auction, on it went to the same pattern: we were always outbid on the things we really wanted, and always over-enthused by the things we didn't. After an hour and a half, there was nothing left from our

List A, precious little from List B, and only a few lots left before attention turned to the expensive bee colonies that we knew were out of reach.

'Lot 201,' said the replacement auctioneer. 'A Universal lightweight side-handle radial extractor. Virtually new. Fully equipped. Should really be over £500, but who's going to start me off at £50?'

'It's brand new,' hissed Duncan. 'We'll never get another chance to get a top-quality industrial spinner. It's now or never.'

'But we've got one hive. This thing can spin about 300 pounds of honey at one go. But you're right, we should see if we can get it cheap.' I solemnly raised my paddle at the £70 mark.

'£70 with the gentleman in the funny hat.' I didn't like the way he said 'gentleman' – or 'funny hat', for that matter – but I let it pass.

Maybe because commercial beekeepers didn't tend to come to this auction, the bidding was relatively slow. This was, after all, a device that could deal with the honey from at least a dozen hives at a time and, even though it was brand new, it simply wasn't raising much interest. The bidding crawled over £100, and we both fancied that its bulky, shiny enormousness was ours for the taking.

'Going once,' called the auctioneer, his formality a nod of respect to the amount involved. 'Going twice.' But just as we were expecting him to bring his fist down, a bid came out from our right. It was the boy with the glasses and the West Ham strip.

'£115 from Ryan there,' said the auctioneer. Ryan looked fathomlessly back at us, waiting for our reaction.

And up it went in increments of a fiver, until Ryan finally bowed out of the bidding at £150. We had our spinner, but it was clear from the muted reaction of the beekeeping community that the headline lot had gone to the wrong bidder: that was supposed to be Ryan's from the start. As for us, we had seen and done enough. We settled up at the desk for the £194.50 we owed for our five lots, and took everything back to the car. The spinner itself covered the entirety of the back seats and, purely in terms of perceived value for money, we had to admit that we had got a lot of machinery for our investment.

As far as our objectives were concerned, we had secured precisely nothing from List A, only the book on sex from List B, and an industrial spinner which just about belonged to List C. As for the things we really needed – the suits, the hive tool, the smoker and the spare hive – we had scored a big, fat zero. Added to which, we had parted company with a grand total of £735.50 of our original expenditure budget of £250 so far, and the likelihood was that we would have some fancy explaining to do when we got home.

Just as we left the car park, we noticed Ryan cycling busily back to the main road. We suddenly felt bad for him, and about what we had done. I mused aloud that he was probably using the income from his honey crop to keep four elderly and severely disabled relatives alive, or giving the proceeds of his efforts to the victims of a far-off famine.

'Never mind,' said Duncan. 'He could never have got the bloody thing home on that bike.'

As we passed him, Ryan gave us a cheery wave, which just made things twice as bad.

Having stopped off briefly at the pub to collect our thoughts, we were concerned when we got home to see Caroline weeding in the front drive, precisely where I always parked my car. I had rather banked on her being out somewhere, or painting something in the discreet privacy of her studio. She looked excited to see us, and asked with enthusiasm whether we had managed to get all the kit we were after.

'Sort of,' said Duncan. After 24 years of marriage, I could have told him that this was the wrong answer. A simple 'yes' would have sufficed, after which she would have cheerfully got back to her weeding. She was a science graduate, and science graduates only need empirical certainty for them to be happy. Bring any element of doubt into the situation, like the words 'sort of', and they suddenly get an unhealthy interest in further research.

'What does "sort of" mean?' she asked, taking a closer interest in the unloading process.

We ignored her, and started wrestling the spinner through the back door of the car.

'Is that the smoker?' she asked with unbecoming sarcasm, returning to her weeding. 'Or is it a little case for the bee suits?'

Much, much later and in the privacy of his New Covent Garden office, Duncan went onto the Paynes website and invested a further £181.64 in the purchase of two protective smocks and veils, two pairs of blue plastic beekeepers' gauntlets and a hive tool, bringing the outlay on our new hobby to a running total of precisely £917.14.

'Terminal Five was way over budget,' he emailed. 'And look at it now.'

But I never saw the message coming in, as I was lying in bed reading about the finer points of the honeybee's sex life.

Chapter 4

THE UKRAINIAN

Late April

....

Even the insects in my path are not
loafers, but have their special errands.
HENRY DAVID THOREAU

....

We talk about someone being a 'queen bee', and we don't mean it to flatter.

We mean it to indicate that the person is bossy, officious and self-absorbed, and it is the fate of every community, family and workplace to have their own. The real queen bee is none of these things. She is both the mother of, and the servant to, everyone in the hive. So long as they tolerate her, their every instinct is to nurture and protect her; they will even pre-digest her food for her, and clean up after her. The mood of the colony, and the actions that it collectively takes, are at the command of the pheromones she gives off. But when they stop tolerating her, they will instantly seek her out and kill her. She is the puppet, and they are the puppet masters; it is they, not she, who will decide when she will lead a swarm, and they will half make it happen by depriving her of food so that she is light enough to fly. Hers is a dark world of signals and sisterhood, where the males – the drones – are stingless, powerless, fatherless adjuncts to the colony, killed at a whim, and whose sole function is to be available at some future stage for mating duties. In the autumn, they are cast out of the hive with the rubbish, considered a waste of rations before the long winter. It is a practical world of extreme feminism in which the men are wholly expendable.

The queen is selected, apparently at random, at her larval stage, and fed an exclusive diet of protein-rich royal jelly* that causes her to be different – longer, larger and the only fertile bee in the colony – and she is then capped in a cell specially constructed around her until she is ready to emerge about a fortnight later. When she emerges, she is a virgin queen, unmated and at her most vulnerable; she may be one of a number at this stage, and she immediately knows that she

....

* Royal jelly is a protein-based secretion produced by bees principally to feed a developing new queen. Many human health benefits are claimed for royal jelly, none of which, it has to be said, are clinically proven.

needs to kill any rival in order to survive. When she is more or less fully developed, she will be escorted one warm day by workers (sterile females) to a drone congregation area on her mating flight, and it is almost certainly the only time she will ever leave the hive, unless she swarms at some point in the future. The colony's future depends utterly on the success of this venture, and on her survival during it. Over the next day or two, she will be mated by up to twenty drones, and will return to the hive with enough sperm to spend the next five years laying up to 2,000 eggs a day, according to the season. Once a drone has completed its mating duties, it falls from the sky stone dead, its abdomen ripped fully open.

A good mated queen is the still point of the beekeeper's turning world. Fundamentally, what we do is not much more than queen management.

The warmth of a late spring was on us when Jim turned up unannounced one day, having heard from a mutual friend about the project, and its vast concomitant expenditure.

'So you really are going to keep bees then?' he said.

'I'm thinking of it,' I replied, unwilling to seem committed to something that might yet go wrong, and earn the ridicule of this most quietly competitive of people.

'Thinking of it?' he asked reflectively, looking out at the gleaming new white hive in the field and noticing the recently arrived parcel from Paynes half unpacked in the hallway. 'I can't wait till you actually decide to go ahead and do it.'

He had a point, so I gave him a coffee and took him down to inspect the hive. Jim had a special brand of lightly expressed disdain which I could normally have done without, but, more importantly, he was a mate and he had plenty of previous with bees. The way I saw it, you either got a few well-placed and possibly helpful caustic comments from Jim, or you got an unstoppable wellspring of unasked-for advice from a local enthusiast who would identify you as a cause, and then never let up. After all, this adventure was never about being an expert: it was about trying out something new.

'Good', as Lord Byron said, 'rarely comes from good advice', but it is the lot of the new entrant into any hobby that advice is a commodity in scarily plentiful supply. The discovery that I was now a putative beekeeper unearthed a rich seam of mainly self-proclaimed experts among friends and neighbours, and they couldn't wait to tell me how difficult it was all going to be, and how I probably shouldn't have started in the first place.

'You have three issues,' Jim said, after taking the most cursory of glances into the hive.

'How do you know?'

'Because everyone with a National has them, until they learn not to.'

'Go on,' I said, quietly dreading that his 'issues' would entail yet further expenditure.

'Not enough ventilation. None of these hives have enough ventilation, so you need to make more. Otherwise the bees' breath condenses on the inside of the hive and either ices up or runs down and makes everything wet. And a wet bee is a dead bee.' He suggested a small plan of action, and then moved on to the next issue.

'The queen excluder is a complete waste of time. Small queens can go through it, and plenty of workers decide not to. Result: crowded brood chamber and swarming. Just get rid of it, and learn to work without one.' I told him that I needed to pass this one by Duncan, but would consider it.

'And the cell size of the foundation is too big.' He explained that most foundation sheets came with a cell size that was bigger than bees were used to, and that the extra space attracted the dreaded Varroa mite* to take up residence. He suggested that I find some new foundation with smaller cells. I had been a beekeeper for just long enough to know that for each problem he had identified, there would be another twenty experts who disagreed with his analysis.

....

* The Varroa mite, since 1990 the main focus of a beekeeper's disease prevention work, is an external parasite that attacks both honeybees and their brood. They suck the blood and transmit viruses that can produce deformed bees, and, if untreated, can cause rapid decline in the colony. First discovered in Asia in 1904, it spread first to Africa and then, by way of Europe, to America. Prevention is relatively easy, and extremely important.

Every beekeeper does things slightly differently, and the key is to learn from your mistakes – and be a mighty quick learner.

'Is that it?' I asked.

'Just about. Other than the fact that you are probably the least suitable person in the south of England to be doing this, but it's a bit late to do anything about that, I suppose.'

On the last Thursday of April, word came through from Viktor, the Ukrainian bee farmer, that our nuc was ready for collection.

I happened to be driving down the M40 at the time, and probably only fifteen minutes or so from his farm, but the bond of a shared endeavour is a strong one, and I knew that although Duncan probably wouldn't say anything, he would have been gutted not to be involved at this pivotal point of our adventure. There were few limits to the rewards available to two foolish enthusiasts on a road trip like this, so I avoided the temptation to go straight over there and pick them up.

'Bring Clare!' said Viktor when I called him back to arrange the pick-up for a couple of days later. 'I think I will like her.'

This presented an immediate problem, in that Duncan had ordered the nuc in his own surname, which happened to be Clare, and Viktor had computed from this that his new client was going to be feminine at worst, and beautiful at best. In a way that seemed to be lubricating the deal between us, the prospect of an attractive woman venturing onto his bee farm appeared to be important, so I assured Viktor that I would definitely bring Clare, and that the person in question was, indeed, much more attractive than me.

The night before collection, we went down to the hive with the air of new hoteliers who were just about to welcome their first paying guests of the season. It was an evening pregnant with expectation of the coming summer, birdsong everywhere, vivid green leaf shoots on each tree branch, and grass growing so quickly you could almost hear it.

'Do you think they'll like it here?' asked Duncan. All of a sudden, my ability to suspend disbelief evaporated in my throat.

'You are a 35-year-old consenting adult and parent, in a developed country with all the benefits of a world-class education, and you have just seriously asked me if a group of prehistoric insects are likely to be happy in a large wooden box you have provided for them. I mean, shall we stick up Michelangelo's "Creation of Adam" on the inside of the roof? Or maybe set up a little chill-out tent for them on the other side of the tree?'

But Duncan stuck to his guns. 'You know what I mean. Is it all as good as we can make it?'

So we fussed around for a further 40 minutes or so, strimming away the long grass and pruning the ends of the damson branches that would otherwise impede our inspections and bee-handling. We also erected a small length of chicken wire by way of making an enclosure to discourage the Southdown sheep from getting too inquisitive about their new neighbours; and finally we hauled the trunk of a felled apple tree down to a point a few yards away from the hive, so that we would have somewhere comfortable to park our backsides when the hard work was done. When it was all complete, we got in some practice at sitting on the log, and found that it was every bit as comfortable as we had hoped. Duncan dug out an old Panatella from his pocket and lit it, watching the smoke drift into the branches of the damson tree above us.

'Six weeks ago, I didn't even know you,' said Duncan, whose default setting was more emotional than his big frame and full beard might have otherwise suggested. It sounded horribly like one of the failed chat-up lines I had routinely used in that awkward period between puberty and my late forties. I said nothing, keen to see what would come next.

'Since then, this previously unknown person and I have spent nearly £1,000, the best part of 200 man-hours and god knows how much thinking time, just to get us to the point of looking at an empty white box in a field near the South Downs. Not to mention the beers. And the coffees,' he added.

'Which all makes me quite proud,' I replied, after mulling it over for a second or two. I wanted to add that the addition of a new friend into my life was sufficient justification for everything to date, and more, but then remembered that middle-aged men don't really say that sort of thing, and let it go.

'I'll pick you up at six tomorrow morning,' he said, getting to his feet after a comfortable silence. 'We have a big day ahead of us, and I want to be back for the Norwich match at two o'clock.'

'Relegation game?' I asked, cruelly. But that was in the good old days before I discovered for myself that every match for Norwich is a relegation game in some sense.

'Sod off,' he said, with the air of a man who has just heard a profound but uncomfortable truth, and climbed into his pickup to go home.

If we had been more experienced, there were any number of cheaper ways that we could have got started, but other people's advice suggested that there was no substitute for buying a mated queen from a reputable supplier. The research we had done had also recommended that we bought an over-wintered nuc, on the basis that the queen and a few close friends of hers would have already proved that they were up to surviving the vagaries of an English winter. These nucs would be the product of at least three different existing colonies, which is why they took time between ordering and collecting, on the pleasing basis that while bees from just two colonies would fight, bees from more than two would be too confused to bother, and would just get on with being bees. This is what Viktor had been up to in the time since we had ordered our queen, and the coming pick-up was the culmination of many hours of labour on his part, with the relatively high cost merely reflective of the work and skill involved.

On the way around the motorway system to Viktor's, I gave Duncan a trivia quiz on bees as far as the intermittent signal on my phone allowed me to. During the course of this, we learned that honeybees fly at 15mph, that they make up 80% of all pollinators, that they are the only insect that produces food for humans, and that they flap their wings up to 11,500 times each minute. Every time I came across a fact that I knew he knew, I passed it by, as it is not the duty of middle-aged men to make younger men feel good about themselves. But when I came across something where I was confident that he was ignorant, I would brandish it, Excalibur-like, in his direction.

'How many bees to the pound?' It was 3,500. Which meant that all the bees in our colony, when it was full at the end of the summer, wouldn't even amount to one tenth of either of our weights.

'How many flowers does a bee visit on one flight?' Plug in the correct answer of around 50, then multiply it by the ten foraging flights she might do each day, and you begin to get some idea of the extraordinary scalability of this production line. So when you see that single honeybee flitting around that single geranium flower while you're sipping your morning coffee, you have to multiply that by 25 million just for the day's work for that one single hive. Twenty-five million visits to the plants and trees around you, and that doesn't even begin to factor in the 30 or so other colonies that operate in the same area. When they talk about the theoretical commercial value to British agriculture of bees as pollinators being in the order of £700 million each year, the experts have arrived at the figure by mathematical calculation, not guesswork, and you can't help but be in awe of the work that they do. The bees, not the experts.

It goes without saying that we got lost. Of course we got lost. No journey in life can be called satisfactory unless you have been lost a couple of times.

We stopped off for breakfast with my hungover son in his student town on the way up, where the only thing that was open that early was a vegan 'all the nutrition-free cardboard you can eat for £4' gaff in the lee of a raised bit of dual carriageway. Fainting with unsatisfied hunger, we were then deluded into following the satnav to a neighbouring McDonald's, then to an address we seemed to have picked at random, which had nothing to do with Viktor or his farm. We were an hour late by the time we arrived at a small collection of old sheds in a beautiful valley somewhere near Chipping Norton. A man came out into the car park clutching the lid of a beehive, which at least gave us comfort that we were in the right place.

'Where is Clare?' he asked, once I had introduced myself while Duncan was parking the pickup.

'Clare is still in the car,' I replied, truthfully. We then both stared at the well-built, bearded version walking towards us.

'This,' I said proudly, 'is Clare.'

'Wow!' he sighed after a second's reflection. 'In Ukraine, our Clares normally don't have so much beard. Congratulations.'

Viktor had come over to the UK for work about twenty years before, fallen in love with a local, and had gradually been building up his bee farm with her ever since. Viktor did the nucs and the honey, and Lucy did the honey-based beauty products and the looking-after of customers.

'My father is a beekeeper in Ukraine,' Viktor announced. 'I learned by not making his mistakes. That is why it takes two generations to make good beekeepers.'

Duncan and I had promised ourselves on the way up there that we wouldn't mention Brexit, and we wouldn't ask him how many times a season he got stung.

'What's Brexit going to do to your business?' asked Duncan, once Viktor had made us a coffee.

'Brexit. Maybe nothing. Britain, though. She will kill us on her own.'

He explained that the Home Office counts beekeeping as unskilled, hobby labour, for which reason he can't bring anyone in from Ukraine to help him over the summer. Given the aversion that British citizens have to working on the land, and given that Viktor has 800 colonies spread over 40 sites over 100 square miles, all of which have to be individually inspected every ten days from April to August, this leaves Viktor in a fair old pickle.

'Maybe we have to go and work in another country,' he said, all the while looking like a man who had taken to his adopted country like a duck to water. 'It's a shame. It takes man years to get used to working in a new country.' He went on to explain that bees in Ukraine were fundamentally more relaxed and easier to deal with, as the continental Ukrainian weather provided fewer day-to-day changes for them to worry about. And he should know: as the god-father of 40 million bees operating in the vicinity, he had more than enough experience in both countries to make the judgement.

He had put into practice his second craft, carpentry, and had a little sideline making his own hives and the beautiful nuc boxes in which he sold his colonies.

'I can find carpenters anywhere,' he said mournfully, 'because your government lets that be skilled work. But it is not same skill as looking after bees.'

Many people who come from abroad to make their lives in Britain have noticed that, as an indigenous popu-lation, we have more or less lost our connection with the land and, in turn, the land's connection with our food, so it's hardly surprising that the majority of us don't give a damn about bees or what they do. In Ukraine, where the Industrial Revolution and its mixed benefits came along later, Viktor pointed out that they tend to appreciate more the things they actually do have, and celebrate the stuff that comes for free off the land.

We had arrived at the same time as the business end of Viktor's season, the equivalent of a toy shop in mid-December; he was selling about 150 nucs a year to people like us, each one the product of hours of painstaking work. In April and May these colonies would disperse to all corners of the country, freshening up the local gene pool and ensuring that about seven million new pollinators got busy on the vegetation. Viktor used to buy his queens in from Greece and Italy but, because of the climate that their genes were used to, they tended to produce colonies that overwintered less successfully than ones from northern Europe. Now, those that don't come from Denmark are sourced from local Buckfast breeders. He would introduce the queen to a mixture of three or four other colonies, until he had a nucleus colony with a mated queen and could sell it.

The last of the season's nucs would head out of the door in mid-May, and then he was on to the honey, extracting and jarring it himself throughout the season, all to the rhythm of whichever nectar the hedgerows and orchards would provide for him, from the first hint of hawthorn blossom in early April to the last knockings of the borage and ivy in late September.

Then he would sell it off to wholesalers and to local delicatessens. On a whim, just before we were leaving, I asked:

'Could I possibly come and work with you for a day at the end of the summer? Just spend a day learning how you do what you do?'

He thought about it for a moment and then said that I would be welcome, and that possibly I would bring a nice, unbearded 'Clare' along with me next time.

As we were climbing into the car, Duncan couldn't help himself.

'I meant to ask,' he said, 'how many times a year do you get stung?'

Viktor held up his thick and calloused fingers and told him that it was none of his business. It's just not a question you ask a professional.

'Enough,' he said, as we pulled away.

For once, the next bit went smoothly. With the exception of the odd bee rising up in the rear-view mirror, and Norwich being trounced in their relegation match on the radio, the journey was uneventful and we arrived back in Sussex in time to put the colony into its future home.

With our new nuc, it was just a question of removing the six middle frames from the brood box of the hive, and replacing them with the six identical, but filled, frames from Viktor.

The whole procedure took less than five minutes, and left us borderline quietly confident that we had started to master at least the beginner's bit of beekeeping.

In a way, it was all a slight anti-climax. The way our beekeeping had gone to date, you would think that fate might have strewn obstacles in our way, but it managed not to. In what seemed all of a sudden, we were standing in the paddock looking at a hive that was populated by bees, *our* bees. It wasn't quite like standing by the car outside the maternity ward with your first-born in a Moses basket wondering why no one has given you the instruction manual, but it had overtones of it. The significance, though, was not lost on us. Everything before this was play time; from now on it was very much for real.

A few mornings later, I learned a sharp lesson in just how vulnerable our new enterprise was.

I got back from some weekend errand and looked out to the field with the excited eyes of a boy who has a new bicycle and needs to keep looking in the shed to check that it's still there. What I saw was a topless hive, the lid and crown board cast aside onto the ground like a scene from some hurricane-devastated island.

In a world of disasters and real human suffering, it seems to me now rather self-indulgent that I actually felt physically sick at the sight of the upturned hive, but I did. In an instant, everything that we had worked towards and paid handsomely for had gone up in the smoke of some pointless sheep breaking through the flimsy fence and rubbing its stupid backside too energetically against what it presumably thought was an exciting new scratching post. Too thick to flee the scene of the crime, the animal was still standing there looking at the upturned hive, and the mass of bees flying around, as if some fractional signal from its one operative brain cell was telling it that something wasn't quite as it should be. Running down into the paddock with no protective kit on, I was wondering both what could possibly be rescued from the wreckage, and how the hell I was going to tell Duncan.

But nature operates in patterns and rhythms that are strange to humans, and, once I had kicked the sheep out of the enclosure and reassembled the hive, the bees simply started flying calmly back in again, as if this kind of thing happened almost every day.

There would be no call to Duncan, but there would be an urgent message to anyone with half an acre of land in the vicinity to the effect that six Southdown rams were immediately available, delivery included.

Chapter 5

THE REFERENDUM

June

....

Brexit means Brexit.
THERESA MAY

....

I't's not just about drunk Glaswegians.

Say the word 'Buckie', in Hamilton, East Kilbride or Cambuslang in Scotland's Central Lowlands, and you will be inadvertently conjuring up images of street drinking, violence and anti-social behaviour. But the virtually undrinkable caffeine-impregnated fortified wine that was developed at Buckfast Abbey in the late 1890s is not the only gift their Benedictine monks have bestowed on a grateful nation. Over a period of about half a century in an isolated Dartmoor valley where his efforts could not be contaminated by other roaming bees, Brother Adam worked on creating, and then perfecting, a hybrid bee that is still the gold standard to this day. The original aim was to create a bee that was resistant to the parasite that had brutally attacked the abbey's hives over the previous years, but the by-product was to achieve a strain of long-lived, productive, hard-working, clean foragers that were disinclined to swarm. Brother Adam was still working on improving the breed up until his death in 1996 at the age of 98. By the time he had done his work, he had travelled over 100,000 miles around the globe tracking down new varieties of bees that could contribute to his genetically modified perfection.

Finding the 'right' bee can lead a novice keeper into a long and often confusing period of research and discrimination when, in truth, all they really want but are ashamed to articulate is loads of trouble-free honey. Before we called Viktor, Duncan and I had sought advice from various local experts, a digest of which might run as follows.

The German, or North European bee is efficient and aggressive; the Italian bee is polite but idle; and the Carniolan, or Slovenian bee is gentle and productive, but is inclined to swarm. You couldn't make it up. Everyone we talked to had a different view as to what we should have, but the *consensus gentium* of the internet searches inexorably pointed us towards the Buckfast hybrid, and that is what we ordered.

Anyway, it was all that Viktor had on offer, and it was the final piece of the jigsaw in the start of our quest for liquid gold. From now on, it was down to us and our little Buckfast buddies.

～♫

For a day or two, we did nothing – which was, to be fair, always Duncan's preferred option.

Each evening I would get back from work and find an excuse to be in close proximity to the hive, just to view its comings and goings. As the seasons came and went, we found that there was no greater pleasure than to sit on the log by the hive with a mug of tea or a beer, watch the activity and wonder idly what was going on inside. This was man working in close harmony with nature, albeit where, in a very pleasing way, nature was doing 99% of the work.

The 10,000 bees in our new colony would have their work cut out to catch up with the late start we had afforded them, and I wanted to see evidence of rapid progress. In a nerdy way that even I privately found embarrassing, I would set a stopwatch for one minute, and then count how many bees returned to the hive during it. First day, eight. Second day, fifteen. Third day, 35, and so on. Each time, I would send a text of the result to Duncan, and he would text back with some facile bee pun like 'Unbee-lievable!'. After two weeks the movements were up to about 100, and beyond my ability to accurately tally. At this point, I switched to keeping a count of the evidence of the different flowers and blossoms they were visiting: red for the field scabious and rock rose, orange for lime and yew, green for meadowsweet, grey for hazel, and so on. It was easy to spot each colour on the panniers on their back legs as they crawled up the landing board to drop off their precious cargo, and beguiling to know that the honey they would eventually produce for us would be an amalgam of the pollen, nectar and water of every plant or pond that they had ever visited. We had bought the bees too late for the bright yellow oilseed rape, a flower to which the bee gravitates like a politician to a TV camera, and which, due to the speed at which it crystallises, forces the honey crop to be taken earlier.

On the morning of June 23rd, I went briefly down to the hive on my way to vote in the referendum that was to decide the future of our relationship with the European Union. My bees were an eclectic amalgam of Italian, German, Slovenian and all points in between, good and bad, so it seemed particularly apposite that I was going to cast my opinion on the ties that were to bind us in the coming decades. Or not.

Just how 'or not' only hit me when I arrived back from work ten hours later, made myself a cup of tea and then noticed thousands of bees swarming above the hive and heading off over the wall into the neighbouring deer park. It couldn't be true. We had only had them for the inside of a month, and already we had upset them enough for the colony to want to split in two. The queen on whom we had pinned such high hopes was even now probably 70 feet up an ancient oak tree with her friends, remarking on the quality of the fresh air and the view. To make things worse, Duncan had just headed up to London for his night's work, so I was on my own in the business of trying to find and take the swarm. My queen might be exercising her natural instinct in leading half my bees away to found a new colony, but we had spent £150 on her, and the way I saw it, her duty was first and foremost to me.

I found Caroline watching the early news.

'You got a sec?' I asked, as innocently as I could. 'The bloody hive has swarmed and I need someone to help me get them back.' That's the great thing about a marriage; the identity of the mystery 'someone' to share a chore is always rather obvious. Asking the question is merely etiquette.

'But what are you going to do with them if and when you find them? I thought you said that you couldn't put them back once they had left.'

'You can't. But I still have Jim's hive. All I need to do is put some more foundation in, and then we can dump them in that. Might work.'

'Might not,' she said.

'A hundred and fifty quid,' I replied.

'OK. I want a bee suit, though.'

Later on, there was a misunderstanding as to my meaning. I had clearly meant 'They cost me £150', and her understanding was 'Blimey! He's offering me £150 to come and help him find his bees'. But the labour had been secured, nonetheless.

As I set the foundation into the frames of the old hive, I spoke of the coming task as a self-appointed expert to my new apprentice. After all, I had already taken one swarm in my career, and although it hadn't ended well, it was one more swarm than 99% of the population had ever done. Which put me in the top 1% of skilled practitioners of beekeeping, if not higher.

We walked down the road to the park gate, looking like a nuclear decontamination crew in our smocks and veils, and holding the by now familiar cardboard box, sheet, and loppers. All we knew was that the swarm had gone over the park wall, and that the queen's clipped wing meant that they wouldn't have gone far. Bearing in mind that searching for a swarm is a three-dimensional activity, and that this was an old-fashioned deer park with hundreds of mature oaks for the bees to hang off, cluster round or hide in, we assessed our chances of finding them at around 20%, and gave ourselves an hour.

Slowly we plodded in a hundred-yard semi-circle, the centre point of which was exactly opposite where our hive was over the other side of the wall, and looked up into the branches of each tree, and in the hollows of the rotten trunks that were lying on the ground, finding nothing. It wasn't until we were walking back along the wall to the gate with our minds on supper and our hearts no longer in the chase that Caroline saw the ground moving just ahead of where her feet were. The swarm, as it turned out, had done no more than hop over the wall and integrate itself with a load of dead ivy roots on the ground. It took us the best part of the rest of the daylight to get the bees securely in the box, back to the garden and dumped into the spare hive. Unlike Jim's swarm a year ago, I wasn't going to make the purist's mistake of letting them enter in triumph up a clean white sheet; these bees had misbehaved, and it was the unceremonial dump in through the open roof of the hive for them.

Six hours later, at around three in the morning, I woke with a start when the little owl gave a sharp shriek from the nearby tulip tree. For a while I lay in the dark, awake through a sense of unfinished business that I was too sleepy to identify, but unwilling to commit myself to actively thinking about it. Slowly it dawned on me that there were actually two things on my mind, not one: the outcome of the referendum vote, and how the new tenants of the 'Jim' hive were getting on. I couldn't do anything about the latter in the dark, but I quietly got out of bed and went down to the kitchen to turn on the TV and check up on the former. The volume was off, but the expressions on the faces of two prominent politicians, one from each side of the debate, told me in elegant silence that the electorate had gone against the bookies' odds and decided to slip quietly off into the North Atlantic and try things out in a different way. The thought that we were all involved in our own minuscule way in the sweeping arc of history, whatever that may be, eluded my tired brain at the time, and I dropped off to sleep on the sofa, dreaming of enormous bees politely queueing up at a polling station.

I was woken with a stiff neck at six o'clock by a ping on my mobile phone. It was Duncan, reacting to a text that I had sent just before Caroline and I had gone to retrieve the swarm. I had forgotten to let him know, in all the excitement, that we had found and rehomed it.

'Bugger,' it said. 'Did you find them? With you by 6.30.' He finished with a single word that indicated he was in little doubt as to where the fault lay.

As I made a cup of tea, a thought came into my mind. There was a curious symmetry between what half the British electorate had just opted to do, and what about half of our bees had chosen on the same day. And as I drank the tea, that realisation shape-shifted itself into the notion that maybe, if they survived, the captured swarm's hive should be known from now on as 'Brexit', and the one they had left should be 'Remain'. A few days later, when a new Prime Minister had been selected, we duly christened our Brexit queen 'Theresa', and, in honour of the German lady across the water who would presumably be calling many of the shots during our divorce process with the Union, we called the Remain queen 'Angela'.

Then, in the interests of fairness and balance, we named the drones collectively and respectively Boris and Jean-Claude. They would do what they would do but, we thought, come September they will be discarded below each hive's landing board and, in our dreams at least, nothing more would be heard of them.

Never one to underplay a metaphor, I headed down to the newsagent in town in preparation of our next Saturday morning inspection, and bought a copy of the *Guardian* to line the base of Remain, and a *Daily Mail* for the Brexit bees. My job, as I saw it, was to make them happy, and being surrounded with the right things plays a large part in this, newspapers included. In a little section of the shop where the cheap children's toys were kept, I found a little plastic Union Jack, which I instinctively knew that Theresa would like, and a European flag that would similarly delight Angela.

With the right names, the right newspapers and the right welcoming decorations, both hives could be unstoppable.

A newly moved colony needs to bed down, and we had lots of theories as to what might be going on.

Out here in our disunited and disgruntled kingdom, the other Theresa was telling us how it was going to be, what meant what and, above all, that we could apparently have our cake and eat it. In both human and bee worlds we headed fractiously on into the early summer, without being able to predict with any certainty what was going to happen. In the event, history went on to suggest that the bees probably made a better fist of things.

As far as Duncan and I were concerned, admittedly as the two least experienced beekeepers imaginable, Theresa was a mated queen by definition, because she was the one that Viktor had sold us. Something had led her to swarm, for sure, but so long as she and her workers were happy in their new surroundings, there was theoretically nothing to stop her starting to lay again; that is, after all, what she would have done in the wild, had we not recaptured her. This meant that, while the Brexit hive should be fine, the Remain hive was in the dangerous position of possibly containing only virgin queens. Every bee in either colony was Theresa's offspring and therefore currently identical: how the Remain bees would turn out and shape up in the future was largely down to the genetic influences of the drones that mated the virgin queen in the coming days. And a virgin queen needs to get out on her mating flight without delay, at which point she is potential prey to every thrush, swift or swallow in the postcode. And that's before any passing woodpecker has homed in on the hive as a convenient source of protein, or wasps have invaded, or mice. Or a bee virus has kicked in. Or Colony Collapse Disorder. Uncertainty would dog us until the day that we saw brood in each colony, as that would be the sure sign that we had two mated queens on the go.

Night after night in the interim, I would sit down and Google bee facts until I was sick and tired of the whole business; in the morning, I would come down and see from the search history that my last enquiry had been at 1.30am and was 'Do bees eat elephants?', or 'Why did I start this stupid thing in the first place?'

Mr Fowler had been right: the pleasure is all in the handling of the bees.

Undomesticated honeybees get along just fine, and have done for millennia. Like most of the insect kingdom, they are extraordinarily robust, battling through the seasons, rain, cold, wind, shortage, drought and even fire.* The wild colony adjusts to life as it finds it, and reproduces itself when it needs to, and when it can. It is only when it comes into contact with *Homo sapiens* that the complications start, and only then when *Homo sapiens* wants to adapt the way that they do things to suit his own ends.

---

* Rather wonderfully, all three hives of bees on the roof of Notre-Dame Cathedral in Paris survived the inferno in April 2019. They were far enough from the direct heat not to be incinerated, and they don't get particularly affected by smoke: it just makes them a bit drunk. Forest fires, after all, are all part of their genetic experience.

In the spring and summer, each frame of the brood box needs to be inspected every seven to ten days in order to be able to see the various potential troubles coming, and to take the right preventative action. More frequently than this, and the bees get set back at least a couple of days each time, which means less honey; less frequently, and the trouble has already happened by the time you look, and you are no longer in control. It's mainly about the life cycle of a queen cell.

So we developed a Saturday morning routine which would, in theory at least, begin at eleven o'clock and finish about an hour later with a diligent writing up of notes in the Bee Book, and a celebratory beer from the fridge. Once we had kitted ourselves up in the protective gear and gathered all the bits and pieces we needed for the inspection, the ceremonial lighting of the smoker would take place. Depending on which one of us was in charge, it could take anywhere between five and ten attempts to get the thing billowing out thick clouds of cool, opaque smoke. Sometimes whatever fuel we were using was too dry and sparse, and it would just burn with a searing flame, scorch a hand and be gone in a minute; other times, it was too damp, and we couldn't get it going at all; then it would be too windy, or we would run out of matches, or we would swear too loudly and bring next door out of her kitchen to see what was going on. Without question, lighting the smoker was the biggest technical challenge we faced in the first year.

'It would be easier just to light a cardboard box of newspapers upwind from the hive,' Duncan had once said in frustration.

However, once the smoker was alight, we would be in business. A waft of smoke in the entrance hole to confuse the guard bees, and then a waft through the half-open lid to send the message to the rest of the colony that it was time for the Saturday morning forest fire. At this early stage in our careers, we didn't have a super (the smaller box for collecting the surplus honey) attached to the top of the brood box; we wouldn't have one until there were enough bees in the hive for the crowdedness to warrant it. So our job was simply to go through all eleven frames of the brood box, and see for ourselves what was going on.

When we first started, and to an extent even now, there was a thrilling blend of elemental excitement and fear each time that lid was fully lifted. The sheer amount of moving life in one small space; the rising and falling of the bees; the buzzing of the attack bees having a go at our veils, oblivious to their own approaching deaths if they stung. There are the hidden patterns, and the crush of body on tiny, unseen body; the wriggling thoraxes coming out of the drawn foundation, and the sense of many, moving as one. There is nothing in routine human experience that prepares us for the sheer weight of dark numbers and crawling activity, nothing in a view of the outside of that calm white box under the damson tree that suggests quite how much is going on inside it.

Partly in childlike fascination, partly in horror movie mode, the novice beekeeper has to suspend the prevailing disbelief that they will be safe within their smocks and veils from the lethal effect of a thousand potential stings. For some it is too much: they never get used to it, still less enjoy it. They become the craft's nearly men, and you can tell them by the hives rotting away at the bottom of their gardens, and by the wistful look on their faces every time they see a pot of honey.

It never ceased to amaze us in the early days how the mood of the hive, of each hive, could change dramatically from day to day. The colony that had been so chilled it was almost horizontal the weekend before, could almost be relied upon to be super-aggressive the next time we checked them, and vice versa. Gradually, we learned not to try to inspect them when there was rain in the air, or a high wind, or a cold front moving through. The ideal conditions were warm, still and sunny (which they liked), in the middle of the day (when most of them were out 'shopping'), and when they were fundamentally happy with life (which was the difficult one). On the worst days of all, we simply abandoned the inspection half-way through, put everything back together again, and beat a hasty retreat to the shed in the company of a dozen or so suicidally inclined outriders.

In the weeks after the referendum, Duncan and I slowly learned the drill and some of the tricks of the trade. And, even when we didn't, we were both drawn from that gene pool of men who would rather state confidently an opinion about whose truth we had not the faintest idea, rather than the much smaller one that admits they haven't got a clue. It seems strange now, but it got us by at the time. At one stage, we asked Jim to come and give us a masterclass, but he announced that in all his years of beekeeping he had never once inspected a hive, trusting instead in the long-term ability of bee colonies to regulate themselves.

'It's all about Angela getting shagged,' said Duncan, breaking the spell one morning. 'That's why we're here, isn't it?'

I might not have put it quite like that myself, but he was right. And not just shagged once, to be crude, but about twenty times. In pursuit of this end, she would head out with her escort of worker bees one morning on what could well be the sole expedition of her life, and which had a 20% chance of ending with her death. If all went well, she would fly to a local drone congregation area (DCA) and be the benefi- ciary of the services of up to a dozen drones, each of whom would die a horrible death for his troubles. Although mating flights tend not to be longer than half an hour, they have been known to spread out as far as ten miles[1] in search of a suitable DCA, throughout which time the queenless colony back in the hive is at its most vulnerable; lose her at this stage, and they effectively have nowhere to go. Assuming all goes well, she has the ability within her to produce anywhere between two and six million eggs after this process. It is little wonder that her escort flies above and alongside her to take the hit in the event of attracting the unwanted attention of an insectivorous bird.

And we would only know that Angela's trip had been a success once we spotted new brood in the Remain hive.

Matt Frei once described the family unit as 'Italy's secret shock absorber' in times of social upheaval.[2] Thus it became for me and beekeeping.

At a time when I was increasingly footloose in my career, with my children leaving home and the joyful secrets of middle age still cunningly disguised from me, beekeeping became a secret shock absorber to the other parts of my life. And this wasn't the only Italian influence on my new world of brood and boxes, larvae and landing boards; in a nod to the Slow Food Movement that was established in Rome in 1986 as a reaction against the first McDonald's outlet there, I felt that there were fewer foods on earth slower than my honey. The deeper I got into this thing, the more I found myself being led off in a direction of less frenetic pace, more care and respect. There was no way to rush a bee; she just did what she did, over and over again, and she did it to the natural rhythms of an English summer, the natural dictates of the world around her. It was as far as you could travel from my other world of artificial commercial deadlines and shrinking margins. The customer could shout as loud as they wanted for as long as they cared: the honey would come in its own good time. Or not.

If I wanted a mere pot of honey, I could just go to a supermarket and buy it. If I wanted a decent jar of artisan honey, I could go to a delicatessen. If I wanted to specify heather honey, or apple blossom, I could travel to Scotland or Somerset and pick it up direct from the beekeeper. But there was something vastly, elementally different about what we were trying to produce from our own *terroir*.* Fundamentally, in a process of ancient alchemy, we were starting to distil the very view around us into something tangible, golden and exquisitely tasty.

As with a tomato lovingly grown in a London window box, or cider apples pressed out in a west Dorset shed, what we were embarking on was much more than mere food production. By involving ourselves in a process half as old as civilisation itself, and by enthusing those around us, we were doing our tiny bit to inch the door back shut in the faces of the people and corporations to whom food was a product rather than a life force, a spreadsheet of gross margins to please the institutional shareholders. Sooner or later, anyone

....

* A word stolen from the French wine industry that brings together all the elements of an area (e.g. climate, geology, elevation, farming practices, etc.) as a perfect descriptor of its food products. It has no English equivalent.

with a soul will campaign for or against something or other in their lives, even if only to annoy people of a different mindset. If it turned out that our campaign was against the men in suits who filled everyone's children with salt, sugar and monosodium glutamate, then so be it. Once we had got rid of our own suits, there were no limits to how subversive we could be.

Philosophically, there was a deeper element to all this. The more we learned our craft (be our efforts ever so amateurish and accident-prone), the harder it became to hide ourselves from the plight of the honeybee and its close relatives. All human progress has in its background some equal and opposite natural reaction, in this case the destructive way we build on, farm and manage the land, and our little colony both encouraged and enabled us to be foot-soldiers in the coming battle to help bees thrive again. And sometimes you achieve more as a foot-soldier than as a general.

Slowly, Brexit and Remain developed their own underlying characteristics.

Unsurprisingly, in the early days Remain seemed out of sorts and depressed. Whatever their minds were on, it was not the business of creating honey. Mooning about listlessly in the area of the landing board, they stung at will, and an active imagination could just about hear them saying that what had just happened was an act of economic self-harm without precedent, and that no good would come of it. Conversely, Brexit was cocky and aggressive. All their flights in and out seemed to be faster, as if directed by some more urgent instinct, and they appeared to be settling quickly into their new regime. Certainly, they were easier to work with for the first few weeks.

(Gradually, we would begin to see physical differences between the residents of the two colonies, to go along with the behavioural ones. Each worker bee gets half her genetic material from her mother and half from her father, so much would have depended on the make-up of the blokes in the drone congregation area where Angela went to be mated. The bees in Brexit became uniformly darker than those from Remain, or at least the majority were, so we fancied that we could identify one worker from another as she foraged in the lavender, roses and sweet peas of our garden. What we were thinking was impossible to prove outside of a laboratory, but we came to the conclusion that Angela had ironically run into a light-coloured Italian strain, rather than the long-tongued and darker Carniolan one, and had found them fit for purpose. Maybe the Italians had simply charmed her more than the humourless Germans, and she had voted with her feet, the saucy old girl.)

Then, on the fourth Saturday, it happened.

Duncan's younger eyes were scanning the central frame of the Remain brood box when suddenly he yelped.

'Brood!' he said. 'New brood! Look! Just over where my finger is pointing.'

I looked, and there it was.

'Seems like Angela got shagged after all,' I said, immediately regretting the coarseness.

New brood remains uncapped by wax for only about nine days, which meant conclusively that what we were looking at must have been laid long after Theresa had led the swarm away a month before. Which meant that it couldn't have been her – it must have been Angela. It didn't matter if Angela was already a mated queen back then, the important thing was that she had kick-started her life's work of egg-laying. From this point onwards, we should be gaining more than 1,000 bees a day as she worked her sinuous way around the mysterious, dark yet golden passages, until the point that our hives were as busy as the ones we had hitherto seen only on YouTube instruction videos, hosted by bizarre people in lumberjack shirts. Duncan's yelp represented one of those pivotal moments in life where the efforts that have been applied into the unknown start to bear fruit, and where we begin to understand that we are not completely incompetent. And understanding that you are not completely incompetent is a specific male need, up there alongside the need to belong.

Three feet away from each other in the northern shade of an unproductive damson tree, we had two healthy queened hives. Far from costing us dear, the referendum swarm had doubled our potential.

A Rubicon had been crossed, and from being people who merely *talked* about beekeeping, we had officially become people who actually *did* it. A thousand things could, would and did go wrong from here on into the middle distance, but we had two hives, and our initial aim of at least one pot of honey out of our apprentice season was one step closer to reality.

Chapter 6

A POT OF HONEY

August

....

Happiness is a butterfly which, when pursued, is always beyond your grasp but which, if you sit down quietly, may alight upon you.
NATHANIEL HAWTHORNE

When you go after honey with a balloon, the great thing is not to let the bees know you're coming.
WINNIE THE POOH (A.A. MILNE)

....

The early autumns of my rural youth consisted largely of finding that Mrs Granger had got there first and stripped the hedgerows, and I hated her for it.

First to the blackberries, as soon as the early fruits had swollen their way from hard red to soft black; first to the rosehips at the very point their redness started to shine suggestively through the maple and hawthorn hedges; first to the field mushrooms where they emerged out of the shaded soil of our secret valley; and first to the sloes the second the initial frost had started to split their skins. And from these she would churn out, respectively, jam, jelly, pickles and gin in industrial quantities. Sometimes she was joined by Mrs Powell and Mrs Wilson, antique locusts advancing remorselessly through the countryside. Mrs Granger traded deviously on the one commodity she had that we didn't – time – and we children increasingly fought back with the area of her greatest deficiency: height. Four foot six in her slippered feet, and born when Queen Victoria was on the throne, she turned out to be too short, and too old, to reach any higher than a ten year old, and ultimately it defeated her. One day I saw her in a wheelchair outside the village hall, and knew immediately that the hedgerows were mine again.

In penance for the evil thoughts I harboured all those years ago, hers is generally the first apparition before me as the sun starts to set ever further to the south at the closing of each summer. And it was she that I was thinking of one Saturday morning when Duncan walked portentously into my kitchen and said:

'Come on, mate. Honey time.'

In all these months of beekeeping, honey had been like some will-o'-the-wisp out on the moors of our imaginations, forever just out of reach. Sometimes we wouldn't dare to talk about it at all, lest doing so placed a curse upon our efforts. But, as every beekeeper realises at some point in their career, having a couple of hives lying about the place is to erect a metaphorical neon sign high above the garden saying 'Honey! Shortly to be available here'. You may not wish to talk about it yourself, but everyone else does. Honey is the price that you are expected to pay for boring them with your stories of re-queening and Varroa treatments.

We were following in a long tradition. There is evidence that the first restaurant threw open its doors within Minoan culture some 3,600 years ago. And that it had honey on its menu. Among the archaeological proof of the wider European historical realities of bone soup, burned bread and bog butter, you will find evidence of honey being eaten for over 10,000 years, which means your great × 300 grandparents were gorging on something that would be very recognisably what you yourself had for breakfast this morning. And, unbelievably, if there were pots of it around from that era, they would probably still be not only edible, but also pretty tasty.*

* Which makes the two- or three-year sell-by dates on the honey pots in your local retailer just a tiny bit comical.

There is a rock painting near Valencia, in Spain, from about 8,000 BC, which depicts a human robbing from a honeybee colony; the fact that the human is carrying an implement that looks very like a smoker of today, suggests that the practice was not in its infancy even then. References to honey abound in history: buried in the pharaohs' tombs, in the Old Testament (Israel was described as a land of milk and honey), and as a healing balm for soldiers of the Roman army. It is mentioned in the Koran, in connection with Hannibal, and in the story of John the Baptist. It was used as a sweetener, a gift to the gods, a medicine and even an embalming agent. The bees that made it were emblematic in some cultures, and the activities associated with beekeeping became central to the monastic life in early Christianity. Indeed, honey is significant in most of the world's principal religions: in Christianity as an offering; in Islam for healing; in Hinduism as part of the birthing ceremony; in Judaism as representing newness; and in Buddhism as nourishment. It appears in the art of the Egyptians, the mythology of the Greeks and the education of the Romans. Pythagoras attributed his long life to its benefits, and Pliny the Elder called it the 'sweat of the heavens'.

Much as we have no idea how and when the first human being looked at an egg coming out of the back end of a medium-sized bird in the forest and said 'I think that might be pretty good with my breakfast', we do not know specifically how humans first domesticated bees. We know that around 4,000 BC, the Egyptians started to keep them in cylinders of hardened mud, and that they even moved them up and down the Nile by boat following the blossoms in their season. We know that further south in Africa, they used hollowed-out logs hanging off trees much as they do today, and that other cultures have used materials as diverse as cloth and wickerwork. And we are also aware that it was an area remarkably free of technological advance all the way up to the mid-nineteenth century when the moveable-frame hive was invented.

Duncan and I were shoe-horning ourselves unceremoniously into those 300 generations of history, uncouth impostors in the quiet, monastic traditions of the craft.

Our knowledge base had moved on from our starting point ('honey is just stuff that bees make') to a more detailed notion of what it actually is, and why it comes in so many varieties. We learned that it's basically no more than plant nectar that has been digested and, how should I put this delicately, vomited up a number of times by the various bees through whom it passes on its way to the cell in the foundation where it is stored. It can be so light in colour that it is almost like a diluted cordial ('water white'), or as black as treacle ('dark amber');* it can be as runny as a cheap olive

. . . .

* There are 40 official shades of honey colour. As a rule of thumb, spring honey is light, summer honey is golden, and autumn-harvested honey is darker in colour and sharper in taste.

oil, or completely crystallised. It can carry the flavour of one dominant flower, or be a genuine 'wild-flower' product that has been made by bees that have foraged over a wide area. Everything depends on the flora of the area within three miles of the colony, and to a certain extent on when the beekeeper chooses to harvest it.

The responsible rookie beekeeper is normally content in their first season to leave the honey in the hive for the purpose for which it was designed, feeding the colony during the harsh and barren months of winter, but responsibility was never going to be a major attraction for Duncan and me.

Caroline, on the other hand, whose training and disposition made her simultaneously more informed and more pastoral than the two of us, was all for leaving the honey *in situ* and gradually winding down the operation through the autumn, until the point when our industrious tenants could huddle cheerfully together in the middle of the frames, telling stories of bygone days, and every now and again reaching into the larder for the bounty of the previous summer.

'Sod that!' said Duncan one morning, when Caroline once again mentioned leaving the bees with the honey they had made.

We needed the physical evidence, even one pot of physical evidence, to justify the resources, money and time we had pumped into the project, and the publicity we had given it. For all our delight at the natural routines of our new hobby, we were still representatives of the instant gratification times in which we lived, and we knew that we could replace what we had stolen with any amount of sugar syrup or bee fondant when the autumn mists rolled in, be they ever so fruitful. The important thing was to have something to show for it.

The process of collecting your honey starts about 24 hours beforehand, when you need to insert a board and a one-way bee escape valve between the super and the brood box. This means that, by the time you get to removing the super the next day, it has virtually no bees left in it, since any that have gone foraging have not been able to regain access to it. If you don't do it, you will find that about 20,000 of your tenants are taking a very close interest in why you are trying to take them and their honey to your kitchen, and are expressing their views on the subject forcefully. Paynes also sell a little soft bee brush to gently sweep away the stragglers, but you can save the postage and the £7.62 by breaking off a few bits of bracken and using that instead. The key is to end up more or less on your own as you head into the kitchen.

By this point, we were pretty adept at handling our bees, and we managed to get the super off the hive and across the garden to the kitchen table without attracting the attention of any more than a handful of passing wasps. Only then did we appreciate the chasm between the enormousness of our industrial spinner and the tininess of the amount of honey we actually had. There were two frames full of honey, say enough for eight or nine jars, and yet we had the capacity to extract at least 250 litres into our new and expensive toy. Somewhere in Sussex, we thought, Ryan would be peering myopically into his tiny spinner and wondering how the hell many times he would have to fill and empty it in order to take the bounty of his 24 hives. 'Tough,' said Duncan. 'He should have continued the bidding.'

'Are you sure it's big enough?' asked Caroline, while taking a load of sterilised jars out of the dishwasher. I wanted to say that sarcasm didn't suit her, but thought better of it, as it did.

Duncan had brought along his two young sons to watch the extracting which meant that, while we couldn't swear the way men normally like to do when they are attempting complex things that are beyond them, the whole adventure would take on the sheen of pure wonder that gets reflected from a child's eyes when something magical is going on. Their presence turned the whole thing from a process to a piece of theatre, which was good in the sense that it made us happy, but bad in the sense that it also made us show off.

Depending on your level of expertise and your attention to detail, the process of extracting honey needs up to seven pieces of kit, and has two end products (honey and wax) to look forward to. For our part, we only had two pieces of kit (extractor and jars) and one end product (honey): modesty of expectation would be our watchword until one day it wasn't.

Before the frames went into the extractor, they had to be uncapped, a relatively skilled job that entails removing the wax caps with which the bees seal their honey. This is best done by a hot (i.e. electric) knife, and by someone (Duncan) with about four times the attention span of me, otherwise you lose too much honey, at one end of the scale, or have jars full of wax deposits, at the other. The frames are then put into the spinner (me) which is closed up (Raef) and spun as hard as humanly possible (Monty) until all the honey has been thrown by centrifugal force out of its cells, and via the walls of the spinner to the floor of the extractor. At this stage the purist (Caroline) would filter and re-filter the honey through sieves until completely clear if we let her, and then pour it from a measuring jug into the sterile jars below. Whatever they say in the books and videos, there are two parts of the process that are massively more fun than the others – spinning the extractor, and slowly filling the jars. Which is why everyone wanted to do them.

You will remember our checked-shirt friend from earlier videos. He, of course, would have the whole thing neatly set up beforehand, and would follow a calm, quality-assured process until he had 60 jars of clear honey out of his single super, which he would then show to his delighted wife, who would say something like 'Attaboy, Chuck!', and that would be that, bar the fade-out music of Lynyrd Skynyrd's *Sweet Home Alabama*. End of video. Here's what he *wouldn't* have to cope with:

1. Not having an electric hot knife, and therefore having to use a blunt kitchen knife in its place.

2. Duncan getting a call from his wife Luzaan half-way through his de-capping, saying that she had locked herself out of the house, and could he come back down the hill and let her in.

3. One of the resident wasps stinging one of the visiting children when they trod on it in their bare feet, and then spending fifteen minutes of third-party distress looking for the Waspeze that turned out to be in the little bowl of elastic bands that someone had hidden on top of the fridge the last time a small child came to visit.

4. Having a Jack Russell attack the spinner while in use, on the basis that it was a big noisy thing that had invaded the house and needed to be killed, despite the fact it was 30 times her size.

5. Having a second Jack Russell attack the first, on the basis that it is generally more rewarding to support the underdog (the spinner), enjoy a good conflict and then knock over and break three of the jars in the process.

6. Discovering that the entire ill-fitted foundation of one of the frames had collapsed in on itself in the spinning process, and had left a load of wire and wax in the honey at the bottom of the extractor.

7. One of the well-meaning children putting the remains of the broken frame on top of someone's recently completed

passport renewal form and endorsed photographs, and then leaving it there so that the honey could drip gently down onto the paperwork.

8. A man from Parcelforce ringing the doorbell for a signature at a critical point.

'There is nothing impossible to him who will try,' said Alexander the Great, though possibly not about making honey, and deep on into the morning and early afternoon we persevered with our dream of attaining the first mythical pot of Upperfold Honey.

Uncapped and spun out, it lay there as a glistening pool at the very bottom of the extractor, looking slightly inadequate in its huge surroundings, and we dipped in a flattish ladle and took out enough honey for us all to sample. To say that our positive tasting notes were the result of knowledge and deep thought would be laughable: we would have given it five stars whether it tasted of tequila or tarmac. But for Duncan and me, who had been immersed in this world for the last six months on and off, that first insertion of those teaspoons into our mouths was close to a religious experience. For a second or two, it seemed impossible to me that our simple equation had worked:

Hive + Viktor + Swarm + Paynes + Auction + Inspections + Research + Resilience + Beer – £950 = Small quantity of honey

The immediate challenge was that the small quantity of honey was still down in the bottom of the extractor, not yet in jars, and that our cute idea of not bothering to filter it was rendered null and void by the presence of the corpse of the collapsed frame in the middle of the pool. If we decanted it straight into jars at this point, there would be a large amount of detritus swimming around which wouldn't produce the desired effect of competence.

We rigged up a vertical Heath Robinson system, whereby the huge extractor stood on the kitchen table, with a sieve hanging off its tap which, in turn, was overhanging a large jug on the chair below. At the moment of truth, Caroline ceremoniously turned on the tap and we all waited to see how beautiful the flow of liquid gold would be as it made its slow, viscous way into the jug, and how it would all unfold.

The answer, in short, was it didn't. The quantity of honey we had produced was so pathetically small that it didn't even come up to the level of the bottom of the tap, one inch above the base of the extractor, which explained why nothing was coming out. I went off and got some weighty old encyclopaedias that were sitting by the front door waiting to go to the charity shop, and propped a few of them underneath one side of the base of the extractor. It was still not enough. By the time we had actually got a flow going, the extractor was at such a precarious angle that it needed both Duncan's children to hold it and thus prevent it from crashing onto the floor below.

'This is boring. Why can't a grown-up do it?' asked Monty. 'I thought you said this was going to be fun.'

'Grown-ups have got more important things to do,' said Duncan tiredly. Twenty years of my own parenting experiences told me that this approach wouldn't work, and nor did it deserve to.

'What, like sitting around getting everyone else to do the work?' came the innocent reply. 'And drinking beer?'

Any potential unpleasantness was headed off by an excited squeak from Raef, who had spotted the first golden stream flowing slowly through the tap and down into the sieve below.

'Look!' he said. 'Honey!'

So, spellbound, we watched it flowing down into the sieve and gathering at the bottom until there was enough there to cause a flow through the thin mesh and down into the jug below. This was the real thing, our personal view of Eldorado as we crested the Andean ridge above. For a minute or two no one spoke; nothing could be said that would add to the beauty of what we were observing. The light streaming into the kitchen gave the honey an almost luminous quality like the fine tracery of a sunlit cathedral window.

Once that was done, it was just a question of re-decanting the honey into jars, a job that I was allowed to do. There was a basic skill in tipping the jug forward just enough to keep up a constant flow, but not so much as to let the contents drop in an ungainly glob and be impossible to stop before the jar was full. Right up to the brim, that's what they said in the textbooks, and that's what we did. By the time our seventh jar was half-full, we realised that that would be the last one we could complete: the little bit that was left in the jug would go in a saucer and would be eaten there and then while everyone present was still in the moment. Then all we had to do was keep the jars tightly sealed, out of direct sunlight and in a room with a reasonably constant temperature.

Duncan brandished our notebook and wrote down the details of our harvest for posterity. 'Seven pots', it said, alongside the date. 'Dark, golden brown, and very tasty.' Winnie the Pooh would have been proud of us.

'Three for you, and three for me,' he said. 'Who gets the seventh one?'

There were many candidates for the honour of that final pot: neighbours, family, friends, people who had been fundamentally supportive rather than deriding our efforts. But the significance of the gift made it somehow especially important that we chose the right recipient. The answer came unexpectedly into the house on a radio signal that carried a phone message from one of our cricketers. I had known that he was going into hospital for some tests on a balance problem he had been experiencing since a bike crash some weeks ago, and I had asked him to let me know in due course how it had all gone. This was partly out of concern for his welfare, but more out of the possible need to replace him in the following weekend's team sheet. We had been too busy and noisy in our extracting work to hear my phone ring, so it was only when I noticed a missed call and message that I actually listened to it. The voice was flat, and I walked out of the kitchen to listen to what seemed likely to be at worst one vacancy to be filled for the following match.

'You asked me to call. Not good news, really. The balance thing seems to have been nothing to do with the crash, and everything to do with a tumour on my brain. Big one. Sadly inoperable. They mentioned the word "palliative" which is not at all what I was expecting. Bit of a bastard, in fact. Anyway, just thought I'd let you know. Tell anyone who you feel needs to know. Not much more to say. We're off for a stiff drink. Cheers.'

I looked at the phone for a second or two, as if the message was the device's fault. I felt that familiar sick tug in the stomach, and visualised my friend sitting down to make the call. By the time I went back into the kitchen and suggested that the kids went out to the trampoline as a reward for all their hard work, both Caroline and Duncan knew something was up.

'Well I guess that sorts out the seventh pot, then,' said Duncan, after I had told them the news. Which it did. We drove it over to them the same evening, and left it on the doorstep with a small bunch of flowers that Caroline had put together.

And, while it sadly didn't sort out any medical miracles in the long run, there was an indefinable feeling between us that, in gifting a tiny bit of that happiness into a desperately bleak situation, our bees had made their first really useful contribution to the wider world.

In some culture on the planet, honey will stand for uncomplicated love.

A few days later, I took advantage of a break in the rain to see how the residents of the Remain hive were dealing with the fact that their winter food source had been robbed. Lines of thin grey clouds were scudding through a birdless sky above the garden towards the north-east, as if summer had been kidnapped and dragged off somewhere in a car boot.

Down on the limestone paving slab that supported the hive, and directly underneath the landing board, were the corpses of 30 or 40 drones,* and I felt a small frisson of gender solidarity on their behalf. Above them, the workers were buzzing in and out of the small opening as they always had, and as if nothing had happened at all; it was just that from now on their colony thermoregulation would gently start to change from keeping them cool to keeping them warm, the outer layer of the swarm acting as a porous structure that

---

* There is a distinct difference between the bulkier, squarer body of a drone and the more classically bee-like worker, which is why it was easy to spot at a glance who was lying there.

could adjust as a group to the outside conditions.[1] A bee born now would live for five or six times longer than its manic summertime half-sister and, if all went well, many of these bees would be here when spring came round again.

All of a sudden, I wanted Duncan to be there with me, just so that we could acknowledge together the end of this our first season, and the start of the next. Chapters in books end with the turning of a page; in life, they just fade from the page they happen to be on into the next, and sometimes you hover over both at the same time.

Chapter 7

TRAGEDY

October

....

*The ruling class is unfit to rule
because it is incompetent to assure an
existence to its slave within his slavery,
because it cannot help letting him sink
into such a state that it has to feed
him instead of being fed by him.*

KARL MARX,
THE COMMUNIST MANIFESTO

....

Death was all around us, and the absence of life she brought in her wake was truly shocking.

A thriving hive of bees is almost a metaphor for the busyness of life, and when the life within it suddenly finishes, the contrasting quietness is deafening. It is like the *sol y sombra* effect on a noonday street in a Mediterranean town, where the light on the sunny side is blinding in its intensity, which only makes the darkness on the shady side that much darker.

Duncan and I stared into the frames of the brood box of the Remain hive, and all we could see were the rear ends of the dead bodies of thousands of bees. They had starved to death long before the first frost.

'They're just bloody insects,' said Duncan. 'But right now, I could weep.'

I knew what he meant. Ironically, we had already started to plan the schedule of work for our first winter as beekeepers, but we had fallen foul of the most basic of errors.

Two weeks earlier, I had gone back to Viktor's to spend a day with him on his farm and learn whatever he could teach me. The deal was that he got a day of free labour from an inquisitive, talkative 50-something, and I got three generations'-worth of accumulated wisdom. When I met him in the springtime, I had got the impression of a man who could teach without lecturing, and listen without judging, and I wanted to tap into what he had to offer before the nights drew in.

As the summer comes to an end, the foraging bees are more and more restricted on where they can find blossom.

Right at the start of the spring, they kick off with hedgerow plants like pussy willow, and with apples and crab apples in gardens and orchards; and at its end, they find nectar among the late summer garden flowers like honeysuckle, *Verbena bonariensis*, Buddleia and Hebe, plants that simultaneously feed the birds with their seed heads and the bees with their flowers. And then, when the last of the garden flowers have withered, they are just left with the ivy. In both urban and rural areas, ivy is the mainstay crop from which bees feed in preparation for the coming winter; nectar produced from ivy, especially old ivy, is of very high quality, and research has shown that bees have to travel less far to find it than they do in the summer, as it is abundant.[1] Something to remember next time you decide to strip ivy off that shed wall, or that tree, to keep your garden neat in the coming winter.

By late September, the hive has probably reduced in bee numbers from around 50,000 to somewhere in the region of half that, before dipping down to a tenth later on in the winter. Because these bees expend much less energy, they live much longer; but because the natural food sources around them dry up almost completely, they are utterly reliant on either what they have prepared and stored in the form of honey, or what the beekeeper has provided them in replacement fondant or sugar syrup, if he happens to have taken their honey. The good beekeeper knows instinctively (as we probably should have done) if the colony is strong enough to allow for most of its 'surplus' honey to be taken, and conversely when he should just leave it in place and wait for a better summer. 'A lie told often enough', said Lenin, 'becomes the truth'; the beguiling fallacy that Duncan and I were good beekeepers had not quite been shattered, but it had a long way to go before it became true.

Once Viktor had got over the fact that I had once again failed to produce a 'Clare', he started to explain the various things he needed to get done before heading off on his holiday. With 800 hives spread over 40 sites in an area of around 100 square miles, and with only one colleague, there had to be a ruthless efficiency in the way he worked. This was especially so if he ever noticed a problem, say extreme weather coming in the direction of Oxfordshire, and wanted to react quickly. Other than exceptionally, it would take him a fortnight to get around every hive, by which time whatever needed doing was probably long past it. And it was out of the question to leave all 800 hives in the same place, as a traditional farmer might do, as there simply wouldn't be the local nectar to go around within the three-mile radius in which a bee operates.

'What are the biggest mistakes a beekeeper can make?' I asked him as we headed out to the first location. He thought about it for a second, and smiled.

'Fighting against nature. That's the main one. And treating each colony the same way. Much of the beekeeper's work is to stop swarms, and yet swarms are how the colony reproduces. So it is bad for us, good for them. The honey is always good in a swarm year. There may be less, but it is good. In Ukraine, we call it "swarming vigour".'

'I have learned,' he said cheerfully as we bumped along in his jeep down the margin of another field, 'that this is not about me keeping bees, but the bees keeping me.' He seemed pleased with this observation. 'Those mistakes my father made in Ukraine. They are mistakes I don't make now. It makes my job easier. Even though it is harder here, and the government thinks we are just ... a *hobby!*' He spat the last word out. 'And that's before they even talk about best-before dates on jars! Or what Varroa treatment we are allowed to use.'

In days gone by, Viktor and his English wife would take their honey to the markets of London, until increasingly expensive pitches and diminishing returns persuaded him to concentrate on selling to wholesalers and retailers in his own area. These days, he looked after the honey and associated products, and his colleague looked after the preparation of next season's nucs. Although the work level died down at this time of year, he still had to attend to the cleaning, sterilising and repairing of hives, and a dozen other mainly precaution-ary actions from predator control to stopping mice making their winter homes among the sweetness of the honey stores.

'In a good season,' he explained, 'four to five hundred hives can be break-even; eight hundred should be good.' Making the point of the scale of his operation, his yard was littered with metre-square containers of industrial sugar syrup from Belgium, eight of them in all, eight tons of sustenance for his 40 million or so bees. I asked him how much they cost.

'A thousand pounds each,' he said. 'And that is just one of my costs in winter.' He ticked the others off on the fingers of his left hand. 'But some of them still think my honey should be free, or cheap, and that my nucs should cost the same as a meal in a pub.'

'Who's they?' I asked.

He smiled, and waved his hand towards London. 'Most are fine. But some. Lifestyle people. They will happily spend £1,000 on getting the hive and the right equipment, but they somehow don't think a bee should cost anything!'

So we drove to some of his sites to feed the hives for the winter. Whereas Duncan and I had no more than little feeding stations on the crown boards in each of our hives, Viktor had made wooden boxes that occupied three-quarters of the area of the top of the hive. Into each of these he poured ten litres of sugar syrup, meaning that a hundred hives would get through a ton of his stores, about double the weight of the entire mass of bees it was there to support. It seemed to me almost impossible that a diminishing number of tiny insects could get through that volume of food, but they can, and Viktor had no intention of coming back to any of these hives again till spring was well under way the following year.

As we bumped along the Oxfordshire lanes with our cargo of syrup bouncing in the trailer behind, little bits of bee wisdom came over to me from Viktor in a happy, osmotic process: how the Buckfast bee happened; what makes a good queen; how to tell if your colony is about to swarm, and what to do about it; what it's like in Ukraine; how thyme oil is the basis of treatment for the Varroa mite. And I found myself demanding information like a child, like that boy in Mr Fowler's garden half a century ago. I wrote things down in my little notebook so that I could force-feed my new knowledge to Duncan, like a penguin returning to its chick. And I knew that days like this were precious indeed, even if they shouldn't be, because they were what I chose to do with my time, and not what I ought to be doing with my time.

Later, when I read up a little more about the British beekeeping industry, it struck me as rather telling that the vast majority of hives are in the hands of people like Duncan and me, hobby apiarists who do other stuff to earn money. Commercial bee farms employ the grand total of 300 people. It is small wonder that the government doesn't care.

But one day they will. That much is certain.

On the way home, I found myself thinking about counterpoint.

Viktor's life was lived to the rhythm of his bees, simultaneously independent and interdependent. It wasn't like some *Country Life* article, replete with soft-focus images of the Oxfordshire countryside that was his workplace, and it was a hard life that was permanently lived in the shadow of things that could go catastrophically wrong, through no fault of his own. But it was a life that dovetailed with the seasons it passed through, day and night, summer and winter, wet and dry, and the end point of it was that, if he did his job properly and had a little bit of luck, he would be there again the following season, maybe bigger and better. Most of what he knew about beekeeping had been absorbed from his father or the day-to-day stuff he did around the farm. He didn't have a PhD to show for it, but he could tell more about what was going on in a hive just by giving it a cursory glance than any professor of agricultural biology. Leaving aside the government, the customers and the weather, I got the impression that he was happy with the life he lived.

I compared it to my own life of early morning flights to distant trade shows, of traffic jams and apologies. I thought of those Chinese factories belching carbon monoxide into the Pearl River Delta sky, filling container ship after container ship with the end product of silicone, plastic, steel, wood or iron that they happened to be producing. And of the ceaseless westward gravitational pull of western consumer for eastern product, of store shelves full of things that no one really wanted, but still someone would buy, and of the smoking landfill sites signifying that moment when 'someone' realised that it was a dopamine kick after all, not a real need, that had driven them to make the purchase in the first place. And of the institutional stockholders for whom 'enough' was simply a six-letter word that had no more part in their lives than the theory of quantum mechanics. And I thought of the one thing we all take as read, and never question: that each year we must grow more than we did the year before, and that each year we will need more landfill sites to get rid of it all. The men in suits will go on bellowing at us through social media and on the television to buy more and more, until one day we start to sink under the weight of the useless things that surround us. And the thing that really hurt was that I was one of them. I had that suit.

When you give the impression of someone who is content in who and what they are, it is a difficult moment when you have to admit to yourself – let alone to anyone else – that you are not. Just as it is difficult to identify that precise moment when you went from being fundamentally at ease with who you are to fundamentally resentful. It wasn't that I cared about ageing, or at least any more than anyone else does. It wasn't that I was remotely unhappy at home, or with my family. It was simply that the asymmetry in my working life had started to block me in. While the work signpost said 'go that way', the values signpost pointed in completely the opposite direction, so I was making a series of decreasingly comfortable compromises. And we were the good guys: all we did was bring things to Britain that people could prepare beautiful food in. The bees had become a small but important part of my 'stop the world, I want to get off' campaign. And, while it probably looked amusing to my friends, inside it was slowly suffocating me.

'No one saves us but ourselves,' said the Buddha; 'No one can and no one may. We ourselves must walk the path.' I had come to beekeeping by luck, but even things that are driven by chance need to have the right conditions in order for them to get going. In my case it was the coming together of three things: having fallen clean out of love with the commercial world I made my living in, having time on my hands after my children had left home, and knowing that my involvement might of itself make a tiny positive difference to the fate of the honeybee. While I didn't necessarily want the life that Viktor led, its simple honesty had much to recommend it.

On a whim, I called Duncan.

'You're getting soft,' he said, after I had spent a few minutes unsuccessfully trying to tell him what I was thinking. 'They're just bloody insects, and they're going to bring us loads of honey.'

With a life expectancy in high summer of no more than five weeks, and with up to 50,000 residents, death is a way of life in even the healthiest hive: after all, it happens around 1,000 times a day. Around 1% of the workers are professional undertakers whose sole function is to remove the bodies of those who die inside the hive, rather than out on the wing. This process is called necrophoresis, and involves the undertaker carrying out the dead body once dehydration has made it slightly lighter than before, and disposing of it at a distance of 50 yards or more from the hive itself. Probably driven by their acute sense of smell, they are perfectly able to prioritise cargoes, and will generally dispose of the older corpses before the new ones, even if the latter are right where they are standing. And don't believe that nature has somehow made this process a simple one: I have watched undertaker bees struggling for up to fifteen minutes to get a sufficient grip on a dead colleague to remove her from the area.

However, all bets are off when disaster strikes.

It was Caroline who suggested that Duncan and I went down to check the hives that Sunday afternoon. She wasn't thinking about the food levels so much as whether we had sorted out the Varroa protection correctly, and had applied smaller entrance holes to prevent unwanted visitors coming in when the weather got colder. The great thing about being married to a science graduate is that they tend to understand the laws of cause and effect, and don't harbour a bucketful of romantic notions that 'things will just turn out fine' if proper procedures are not followed. Personally, I was thinking about lighting the fire and settling down with the weekend papers, but I knew she was right.

Brexit had a few bees to-ing and fro-ing from the entrance hole. We had left the super on, given that we hadn't taken any honey off them, and a cursory glance inside showed that all was well, even if the colony was still pitifully small. We had briefly hatched a plan to merge the two colonies ahead of the winter by the old trick of placing the weaker Brexit brood box on top of the vibrant Remain, with only a sheet of newspaper separating them. The idea is that it takes the bees about 24 hours to chew their way through the paper, by which time they will have neutralised their own tribal smell as far as the other lot are concerned, and therefore not risk getting into an anti-migrant bloodbath once they have broken through. But Duncan had got busy with his button mushrooms and brassicas, and I had been abroad for a couple of business trips, and the intention had never seen the light of day.

Certainly, neither of us had imagined that one of the colonies would starve. The weather was mild and frost-free, and there were still flowers around for the bees to forage. Besides, we had given them a small supplement of sugar syrup when we had taken their honey back in August, more as an apologetic peace offering than in any real expectation that they needed it.

When we opened up Remain, we noticed a few dead bees on both the landing board and the crown board and were immediately struck by the lack of activity. But it was only when the lid was fully off, and we started taking the frames out of the brood box that we could see that 95% of the colony was immobile. And it wasn't until we worked it out for ourselves that we understood that the thousands of little backsides sticking out of the drawn foundation were evidence of a mass starvation, each hole the final port of call of a frantic, instinctive attempt to live, to find the last shred of nutrition before the organs began to shut down. A few survivors flew listlessly around the top of the frames, but otherwise there was only silence.

There were two possible explanations for this but, by the principle of Occam's Razor,* the more comforting one to us – that of a strange disease that was in no way our fault – had to be discounted.

While bees can starve in any month of the year, the autumn is a particularly vulnerable time, since the external food sources are diminishing at a faster rate than the size of the colony, and we were unaware that it can take as little as a couple of days from the colony being seemingly healthy to a state of extinction. The practised beekeeper learns quickly how much honey it is safe and proper to remove from the colony to diminish this risk, but we were still at a very early and shallow point of the learning curve. Equally, a couple of quid's-worth of sugar syrup or fondant would have ensured this never happened, a tiny fraction of the £900 or so that we had spent on getting the Upperfold Bee Farm up and going. But for the present, we had nothing more useful to do than to admit we had made a ghastly mistake, and to learn from it. We had lost more than 50% of our capacity, in that it was the stronger and more productive hive, and we had lost it at

....

* The philosophical principle by which the explanation that requires making the fewest assumptions is probably, and annoyingly, the thing that has just happened to you.

the worst time of year: with our lack of resources and skill levels, there was nothing we could practically do until the start of the new season, by which time it would probably be too late for the bumper harvest that we had in mind.

With the aid of a bottle of sloe gin that we kept down in the shed for emergencies, we sat on a log and went rapidly through all the stages of grief in about fifteen minutes: disbelief, denial, guilt, loss of confidence, anger, bargaining, chaos, resignation, acceptance, recovery. Duncan said the word 'shit' so many times and in so many different contexts that I began to fear his never great vocabulary had disappeared altogether. To make myself feel slightly better, I told Duncan of all the many things that these bees wouldn't now need to go through in the rigours of old age, having died before their time.

'They won't have to get up in the middle of the night to go to the loo,' I said. 'Or not be able to read a menu in a dark restaurant. Or have to turn the television up. Or get ridiculously stiff after a day's gardening. Or take up bridge. Or wonder what happened to the neighbourhood, and where deference went. Or go on about how there used to be trees round here, and how the best bit of a holiday used to be collecting the photos from the chemist. It's not all bad, you know.'

Duncan looked down at his boots for a second or two, lost in a world of private thoughts. I could see that I had given him some tangible things to hold on to in his grief.

'Did anyone ever tell you what a complete dick you are?' he asked, without expression.

Two emotions dominated the coming days. First, sheer guilt that we had taken the entire crop of their summer's work off our bees and then failed to make sure that they had enough food of their own; and secondly, amazement at ourselves that we could harbour these strong emotions for insects, of all things. To the amateur psychologist, it looked perilously close to love.

Not for the last time, we had astounded ourselves by just how much we minded, by how much this wasn't just a couple of bored blokes doing something new.

The immediate problem was a practical one. For psychological reasons as well as ones of good husbandry and hygiene, we needed to dispose of around 20,000 little bodies, and at least sort the hive out for whatever future awaited it.

'What's wrong?' asked Caroline, seeing my face as I went back to the house to pick up some matches and a dustpan and brush. I explained.

'Well, I wouldn't beat yourselves up over it,' she said once she had commiserated, but knowing that I would. 'Just learn the lessons now, find out why it happened and don't make the same mistake next year.'

'Jim will love this,' I said unfairly. 'It's exactly how he said it would end.' As one of life's experimenters, I was super-sensitive to the background criticism that tended to escort failure, at least in my own mind.

Near the hive was a small bonfire that had been gathering hedge clippings and storm-damaged tree branches for the last few weeks, and we decided to give the departed a full Viking send-off once we had reclaimed the frames for cleaning and storing. Viking funerals were a bit of a family feature as far as pets were concerned, and many was the gerbil, goldfish, chicken or rooster who had gone up in a puff of aromatic smoke when my boys were younger. We drew the line at dogs and sheep, but anything else was legitimate ceremonial fuel as far as we were concerned. The sense of doing something unusual and respectful served to soften the blow of loss when the boys were younger, we found, and we only brought the procedure to an end when the sheep got nervous on their own account.

Burning the bees was a more downbeat affair, but soon it was done, and it was then just a case of getting the hive and its frames into the shed to dry them off and recondition them for the following year. It seemed strange to think that only a few short weeks ago we had been celebrating the honey that had been produced by the very bees that we had just incinerated.

'We're going to force ourselves to write this stuff down in the Bee Book,' said Duncan. 'Just to make sure that we remember what we did, and don't do it again.'

We hadn't entered anything into the Bee Book for weeks, months possibly. Initially, I wasn't even sure that I would be able to find it among the detritus of a long-flown summer, but eventually I did. The last entry had been in late July, so there were two months'-worth of blank pages for me to pass over in shame before reaching October. To my surprise, there was already something written into the first page of the month, and to my even greater surprise, it was in my own handwriting. Dimly I remembered jotting down little *pour mémoires* at the start of the season, so that we would have our memories jogged as to what needed doing as we turned over into each new month. I read it and then wordlessly passed it to Duncan.

'Check food supplies every weekend,' it said. 'Never leave them short.'

Chapter 8

IN THE BLEAK MIDWINTER

Late December

....

*People ask me what I do in winter. I'll
tell you what I do in winter. I stare out
of the window and wait for spring.*
ROGERS HORNSBY

....

We got over the tragedy at different speeds and in different ways.

In the case of Duncan, who had twenty years less experience than I had of Sod's Law, this was marked by a renewed determination to learn more and, through the boringly whole-hearted pursuit of excellence, become a better beekeeper. He started re-reading the books we had bought at the beginning of the year, and then endless articles put online by people with an annoying degree of passionate self-assurance and consequently limited friendship groups. Each morning I would come down to breakfast and find the night's harvest of what he had gleaned, staring insolently up at me from my inbox. Most of the time the things he sent were practical, obvious even, but sometimes they were bizarre to the point of weirdness, and I began to wonder whether the vegetation in the market wasn't getting to him. Always, though, they carried with them the strong hint of future investment opportunities.

For me, what had happened to the Remain hive was just another bit of proof that the essential role of middle-aged life was to trip me up and cause mayhem while I wasn't looking. For a few weeks, I approached the whole project with the jaundiced scepticism of a man who instinctively knows that the next cock-up is heading in his direction at speed. As autumn folded into winter, Caroline left the *Collins Beekeepers' Bible* suggestively on my bedside table, where it remained unread, subservient for several weeks to a miserable book on global warming and a hardback copy of *Tintin in Tibet*.

But all of us looked on the Brexit hive differently now, knowing that what had once been the poor relation had now moved centre-stage. Screw this one up in any way, we didn't need telling, and that would be the end of the Upperfold Bee Farm.

After a series of false starts, winter had set in with a vengeance.

Frost cascaded down the hill each morning, nuzzling itself into pockets in the hollows and dips of the garden, insinuating itself into the very stonework of the cottage until everything around reflected the monochrome of utter coldness. From time to time, snow flurries blew across the wall from the park, propelled by winds born somewhere out in Siberia, then settled resolutely in the edges of the flower beds and the hidden depths of the grasses in the field. These were times when logic drove us inwards to the core of the house, to the fires, radiators and electric blankets, just as summer had called us out into the garden and the fields beyond.

This was the business end of the year, where any expenditure of energy not directly connected with finding food was a waste. Standing in the field early one morning, I watched a fox slink through the grass and then melt through the gap below the gate and out onto the road, and I knew that she would only be out there because she had failed to find enough food under cover of darkness. Behind me on the bird table, a pair of blue tits scrabbled for what the bigger birds had left behind, which wasn't much, then scarpered into the beech hedge when a puffed-up blackbird made its presence obviously unwelcome. Out in the woods, fallow deer that had escaped from the walled park over the last few years switched from grass to the relative riches of acorns, sweet chestnuts and bark, and the last of the autumn fungi turned black and died away.

Against a background palette of greys and whites, nature's night shift was getting on with the all-consuming business of survival.

To understand what a bee does in the deep midwinter, you have only to imagine the polar opposite of what she does in high summer. The ten pounds or so of honey that she and her colleagues will get through before the sun has another chance to warm the park wall behind them will be the result of 20 million or so flights earlier in the year, and it is that honey, or a substitute, that will keep them all alive. The summer bees are all dead now; what occupies the centre of the hive is a small cluster that might have been born in late August or early September, and who, with luck, will see things through to the following spring. The queen stops laying, and the useless drones have been kicked out to die before they gorge on rations that the sisterhood feels they have no right to call on. As the temperature plummets outside, they concentrate inwards from four or five frames to just a couple. Bustle gives way to calm, cooling to warming and long foraging flights to short trips to the top of the brood box for food. Everything they do derives from the one sacred aim of keeping the queen alive and well into the next laying season, and the premium they paid in their relentless work over the summer imperceptibly becomes the payout.

Providing they have sufficient food, the challenge for them is to keep warm, and keeping warm depends on the huddle. At the centre is the queen and any remaining brood, while around her the 5,000 or so designated survivors alternately eat honey and then deploy the energy gained into shivering, vibrating their flight muscles but keeping their wings still. With thousands of bees providing the warmth in this way, the core temperature can go as high as 30 degrees Centigrade; the outside layer of bees will constantly swap places with those on the inside, so that the bitter cold and the heat production can be shared around.

To an extent, the bees in my field are lucky. If they were in the USA, for example, their food would now be facing the unwelcome seasonal attention of skunks, opossums, raccoons, bears and, above all, badgers. Here in West Sussex, so long as the bees have won the perennial battle with the wasps each autumn, and so long as a combination of they and the beekeeper have reduced the access points into the hive down to a small hole above the landing board, what they have laid down for the winter should be theirs to eat.

A few weeks after the tragedy, and having run out of space to store it inside, Duncan and I reassembled the newly cleaned, refurbished and repainted Remain hive back where it used to be in the field.

'Are we going to wait for a swarm in the spring, or call Viktor now to order a nuc for April?' he asked. It was a loaded question, given that Duncan was a man who missed no opportunity to buy new kit and enrich the wider commercial beekeeping world. Despite having more patience in his little finger than I had in my entire body, he was curiously impatient in the matter of spending our meagre funds.

'Let's wait for a swarm,' I said, and not just to annoy him. 'If we get a nice early one, we could get a decent crop of honey by the end of the year.'

By 'early', I meant at the very beginning of May. The disadvantage was that the swarm would arrive, if it ever did, a full two or three weeks after Viktor's nuc, and the bees would already have developed the swarming habit. It would be pot luck finding them, pot luck catching them and pot luck persuading them to hang around. In my mind's eye, they would be constantly flicking through holiday brochures deep down in the hive, sorting out their foreign currency and arranging airport taxis prior to buggering off into the wide blue yonder again. The advantage of waiting for a swarm, on the other hand, was that it was free, and there was something elementally satisfying about the completed process of homing bees that have gone back to nature. Duncan and I could also take in it turns to bore people in the pub into catatonic despair, by regaling them with our natural knowledge.

He thought about this for a second or two. 'You're probably right. It slightly depends on whether this lot' – he pointed down at Brexit – 'get their arses in gear. If they do, we can have a good harvest. If they just faff around like they did this year, we'll have to leave them with whatever they make.'

'How are we going to know? I mean, before it's too late to do anything about a new lot?'

'We aren't,' said Duncan. 'Because we can't.' He seemed pleased with the unintended rhyme, and repeated it.

We had stumbled, not for the first time, on one of the core challenges of working alongside nature in its widest sense, and of farming for honey in particular. Nature does what it does, and it knows what it knows. The most skilful angler in Europe can stand for hours on the banks of the most productive and expensive beat of the Spey, in perfect conditions, and can often come away with not so much as a tremor on the line. Whereas someone large and clumsy who has never fished before, Duncan for example, could drop a mass of tangled line and fly into a stagnant pool above the neighbouring sewage outflow and get himself a six-pound salmon for his troubles. It all depends on natural rhythms and pulses plus a whole dollop of serendipity. Hobbies that plug into nature's unpredictability are probably not what you should take up if your school's careers teacher assessed you as a budding nuclear physicist. Mine didn't, so that was fine. Mine had suggested that I forge a career working in a public library so that I learned how to shut up.

The most frustrating thing about beekeeping also happens to be the most alluring. As the beekeeper, you are simply working as close to the grain of nature as you can, replicating what your knowledge tells you are the optimal natural conditions within which bees can live, and make honey. Perhaps you can affect the outcome up to 50%. The other 50%, containing as it does marauding bands of wasps, the Varroa mite, drought, cold, damp, mice, colony collapse, levels of local biodiversity, Duncan, and even some stupid sheep rubbing its arse against the hive, is outside your control.

'Sod it!' said Duncan after a pause for thought. 'Let's get another nuc.'

This was pathetic crumbling in the face of minor obstacles. Like Bunyan's pilgrim, he had reached the fork in the road but he had chosen the path of least resistance. The mask had slipped on that bearded face and revealed a lightweight, a flaky part-timer. For a moment or two I was shocked.

'Gets my vote,' I heard myself saying. 'Can't be bothered to wait around for someone to report a swarm.' How much easier to go to the kitchen, drop Viktor a friendly tea-time email and then wait for three generations of Ukrainian excellence to work its magic with next year's tenants.

'I think we might just avoid mentioning the starvation incident,' I added. 'I don't think he needs to know.'

And without so much as a second thought, our Year 1 outgoings had risen from £917.14 to £1,067.14, taking us to an amortised price per pot that would make even a Waitrose buyer blush.

Once we had ordered the new nuc, we brought out the reinstated Upperfold Bee Farm Book and made a note of the jobs that we needed to attend to between now and the start of the season in March. I had always found that making lists was a wonderful substitute for actually doing anything, and noting it all down for the months of January and February struck both of us as quite an achievement in itself:

1. Check for woodpecker damage. Create some kind of coating or shield that stops the little bastards pecking away at it in the first place.
2. Monitor the entrance for build-up of dead bees, and clear them if necessary. One of the features of thousands of short-lived creatures living cheek-by-jowl in a small space is that death is a frequent visitor. If dead bees block the entrance, it means that the others can't go outside for water, or to take a crap.
3. Check regularly for any signs of wind or weather damage and repair accordingly. Bees are wonderful insulators of a property, but they need a little bit of help if whole pieces of the superstructure rot away, or get broken.
4. Treat the hive in January for Varroa and then check the floor a couple of weeks later to see how badly it had been affected in the first place.
5. Gently heft the hive ('hefting' is the act of simultaneously lifting and judging weight) to assess how the food stocks are doing. If running short, lob them a bit of soft sugar

fondant to keep them going. This is the time of year to try to avoid opening the roof if you can possibly help it.

6. Make sure that the roof is secure against winter gales, by strapping it down to the main hive if necessary. A high wind could get underneath it and lift it away into the night.

7. Plan the following year's strategy, and lay the groundwork for it, ordering new equipment if necessary. Or even if not necessary if you are called Duncan.

8. Use the winter nights to read up beekeeping books, and study for the British Beekeepers Association exams in the spring. As if.

Satisfied that eight action points was a good round number, we called it a day and celebrated with a slice of Christmas cake and some of last year's sloe gin.

'I'm amazed you haven't thought about awarding yourself a Christmas party,' said Caroline, who had been a silent witness to our industry up until this point. 'After all that hard work.' Twenty-five years of marriage had taught me that this suggestion was born in irony and jest, but Duncan innocently seized upon it.

'Good thinking,' he said. 'We'll add that to the list.'

9. Organise Upperfold Bee Farm Christmas party.

We looked approvingly at the new task, until we realised

that its addition had removed the symmetry of the original round number.

'We can't have nine tasks,' I said. 'It just doesn't work. We need another.'

Thus we scoured the outer reaches of the most distant search engines we could find, until Duncan announced with a triumphant shout that he had found the very thing.

10. Learn the fundamental steps of the prehistoric Sumerian winter bee veneration dance, and replicate the Great Oracle Stone in order to perform it.[1]

With only a few days to go until Christmas, we were very aware that we needed to rank this list in order of importance and urgency and, whichever way we looked at it, the Christmas party was the one that needed our immediate attention. The woodpeckers, dead bees and Varroa mites could wait in line like everyone else.

'Most of it can hang on till the new year,' said Duncan as he left. 'But who's ever heard of a Christmas party in January?'

There were important things to consider before we went ahead. Should it be staff only, or staff and their spouses, or staff and their complete families? Should we go for a venue that required us to dress up for the evening, or keep it simple? At home, or in the pub? Would there need to be speeches and toasts? Was it an opportunity for a Michelin-style meal with an eighteen-course taster menu and wine accompaniments?

'What have we got in the account?' I asked.

Duncan checked his phone. 'Nine quid, plus or minus,' he said. 'So possibly not the taster menu.'

In the end, we settled for a two-phase party in my kitchen the following Sunday evening, where Duncan would provide the spirits and I the beer, Duncan the mince pies and I the Cheesy Wotsits. Phase One would include any of our families who had nothing better to do, whereas Phase Two would be hardcore stuff, employees only, that bit where the home truths pour out in an unguarded moment, to be regretted evermore once back in the office. Our sole nod to seasonal decorum would be the provision of a small gift to each other.

I'm not saying that the question of what present Duncan would bring me was keeping me up at night, but I was just a tiny bit proud that the two of us had set something up from zero that actually justified any sort of party, let alone a Christmas one. A year ago, we didn't even know each other.

Duncan arrived with Luzaan and his two boys at teatime on the appointed day.

'Now, we're just staying for a few minutes to have a bit of cake with Roger and Caroline,' she said. 'Because you've got to get ready for the carol service tomorrow.'

'But you said that we could stay around for the party,' said Monty. 'Get the beers in. Like Dad does.'

Glances were exchanged, not least between Duncan and Luzaan, followed by Duncan and me, and finally me and Caroline.

'Show him what you've brought him, Dad,' said Raef.

Duncan handed over two parcels, one of which was more obviously a bottle of whisky than if he hadn't attempted to wrap it at all.

'Happy Christmas, mate.'

I peeled back the paper on the bottle and saw to my joy that it was a sixteen-year-old Lagavulin. He had chosen well, and he had chosen generously, a fact that was already making my £3.95 gift of *101 Insect and Funny Bug Jokes* look dangerously ill-judged.

'That's really kind of you,' I said, meaning it, and searching my mind for something a bit more generous that I could press into action as a replacement gift for him.

'Show him the other one! Show him the other one!' shouted Raef.

'Maybe a bit later,' said Duncan, looking uneasy.

'No, now!' said Monty, snatching it and handing it over to me.

Experience told me that it was going to be pornographic, or vulgar at any rate, and that it was therefore my duty to open it very publicly before the kids went home. They would expect nothing less.

Peeling the paper revealed a thick blue paperback that, in the event, looked distinctly un-pornographic. Even less so when it was fully unwrapped and revealed itself to be my very own brand-new copy of *You Mean I'm Not Lazy, Stupid or Crazy?! The Classic Self-Help Book for Adults with Attention Deficit Disorder*.

'You shouldn't have, mate.' I said. But inside I was secretly longing to be upstairs in bed reading it. No one in the world had more right to give me that book than Duncan, and I couldn't wait to devour its secrets.

Two or three hours later, we were sitting round the kitchen table looking at the wreckage of the £60 Lagavulin bottle and many empty packets of Cheesy Wotsits. In a parallel life in some other part of the house, Caroline was wrapping Christmas presents and watching a repeat of *Grand Designs*.

In the intervening hours, we had fulfilled a strange decision to complete most or all of our ten tasks that very evening, a process that had entailed a series of increasingly pointless torchlit processions down to the hives on the other side of the field.

'I mean, you don't need a torch to heft a super, do you?' asked Duncan rhetorically.

'Probably not,' I said. 'How much is in it?'

'I don't know. I've never hefted something before.' He had a point.

'We'd better open it up and look, then,' I suggested.

But we couldn't, as we had foolishly completed Task 6 (securing the roof down against winter gales) before Task 5 (hefting), which had locked the whole unit together. If we wanted to heft anything tonight, we would have to lift the whole hive off the ground. Given the uncertain state we were in, this wasn't necessarily the wisest move. Bees can be notoriously touchy creatures, and having your house lifted off the ground, waggled around a bit and then thumped back down might not come under their idea of a good evening.

'Woodpecker damage?' asked Duncan.

'None.'

'How do you know?'

'No woodpeckers. And if there are any, they stay in the park. And if they don't, they go over to that telegraph pole.'

'Which telegraph pole?' he asked. But the beam of the torch was too dim, and the pole too far away for me to show him, and it was at this point that we decided to retreat into the kitchen.

In the end, all we physically achieved was to remove a few dead bees from the general area of the landing board, and to lose the shed key. Instead, the magnificence of our efforts lay in the fact that, during that period, we arrived at our entire strategy for the following season's beekeeping activities.

'Three hives is what we'll do, then,' said Duncan alongside an ill-suppressed belch, once we were back at the table.

'We'll have Brexit with the already bees in it,' I replied, my ability to put words in the right order compromised by three hours of Lagavulin. 'And we'll have the Viktor bees in the other one. What's the other one called?'

'Remain,' said Duncan after a long thought.

'And then we'll have a swarm colony, which means we need another hive.'

'Did you know,' slurred Duncan after staring at the lights on the Christmas tree for a while, 'that a foraging bee is better at mathematics than a computer? Or a person who is good at ...' – he searched for the word – '... maths?'

I asked him why.

'Coz the foragers can work out the quickest distance between five different flowers quicker than anyone else.[2] A computer, even. And they're always right.' He paused for a moment. 'Clever bastards.'

'And you get lazy bees. And hard-working bees. And brave ones. And timid ones. And ones that vote in elections. And ones that don't.'[3]

'And do you know that they can navigate by polarised light even when it's not sunny? Or something.'

'Three hives, three colonies, 150,000 bees, 120 pounds of honey. Simple.' I had done the maths, and I knew what lay ahead of us.

We toasted the success of our efforts with the dregs of the bottle, and Duncan got up to walk back home. Lurching towards me to envelop me in a drunken bear hug, he tripped over one of the dogs and ended up for a second or two sprawled on the dog bed with a warm smile on his face.

'To friendship!' he said, got back up and wandered off into the night.

Chapter 9

THE STING

The following April

....

*Fortune knocks but once, but
misfortune has much more patience.*
LAURENCE J. PETER

....

I t's an ill wind that blows nobody any good.

Unlike the previous year, the arrival of spring didn't take us by surprise. When it finally sauntered up the valley at the end of a long winter, wreathed in light winds and mist, we were ready for it.

The chiffchaffs and blackcaps arrived in the garden first, followed by the swallows, but it was the resident jackdaws that made their presence felt the most. After a winter spent holed up in the old oaks in the park, they took to flying around the chimneys with their mixture of raucous call and sonar 'ping'. We would learn what they were up to only when the smoke from the wood burner backed down the chimney and into the house in the autumn.

Out there in the fields, woods, gardens and hedgerows, the plants were getting ready to tempt the pollinators back in after the long gap of winter. Alder, hazel and yew were among the first of the trees to get going, with snowdrops, crocus and dandelion down on the footpaths. Bees can start coming and going by the end of February, but they should be taking to the air regularly in March. This is the riskiest time for starvation in the hive: they have probably used up all their winter resources, but have not yet been able to build stocks up in any meaningful way. Hive checks are done at this stage more by subtle observation than detailed inspection, as it's still probably too cold to allow the open air deep into the heart of the brood box. With recent experience in mind, our bees were likely to be among the best fed in the kingdom for the foreseeable future. All a bee would need to do in order for the whole colony to receive a massive food supplement was to look a little peckish.

When spring came that year, it came in more vivid colours for me, and with a greater sense of urgency, than it ever had before. I would wake up with a sense of excitement that, for all the grim change that might have been reported overnight on the various news channels and websites that were waiting for me downstairs, our bees would be another tiny step nearer to getting back into full production.

I started to notice things like early blossom that I had never registered before, and to think in terms of what my bees would be up to at any given stage in the cycle. Stirring in the middle of her huddle, the queen would be starting to lay brood again, and her colony would inexorably be working its way towards creating another honey store. First in singles, then pairs, then half-dozens, we would see the foragers on the landing board, getting ready to fly or preparing to re-enter the hive. You could tell the difference between the goers and the comers, as the former would have no coloured pollen on their back legs, whereas the homecomers were festooned with it: yellow for the pear and crab apple, red for the snowdrop, orange for the yew and brown for the elm.

And the learning thrilled me, as it had not done since I was that nine-year-old boy. Our beekeeping was just the tip of the iceberg of the ecosystem around us. It was the things that radiated out from our bees that re-awoke a child-like fascination in me. I learned of the co-evolutionary relationship between plants and their insect pollinators, how the habits of one would shape the construction of the other, which would, in turn, shape the physical development of the first; of how the iris is perfectly adapted to benefit from its principal pollinator by how it channels the bumblebee under its stamen at exactly the right height to brush off pollen, and then brush it back on again; of how the scent of flowers is timed to coincide with the most active part of the day or night of the insect that pollinates them. Obvious though all this may have been to anyone with science in their bones, it was miraculous to me.

Winter had also shone a spotlight into my slight feeling that life had not only been passing me by, but had stuck two fingers up at me as it roared off over the horizon to the beach with all my friends in the back of the car. As midlife crises go, it was not even a particularly impressive one. If I had had to define it, it would have been along the lines of 'middle-aged, middle-class, middle-of-the-road, privileged, comfortable, secure, moderate, employed, sane, healthy, white Anglo-Saxon bloke forgets what he was put on earth to do with the rest of his life and minds quite a lot about it'. It wasn't going to have me admitted to the Priory, but it was real enough if you happened to be inside my head at the time.

While never losing the ability to laugh at the caricature I was in danger of becoming, I also could not hide from myself that I needed to achieve little things, *new* things, that I was proud of before I lost the ability to achieve anything at all. And that was the thing about our bees: they had flown into my life as one of those *things*. There I was thinking I needed to become Prime Minister or at least be the possessor of a violently floral shirt, and it turned out that what I really needed was the responsibility for, and company of, a load of relatively grumpy insects.

And the friendship of Duncan. Who, as it happened, was the bearer of some particularly good news.

We had been working away one April morning on kick-starting the Upperfold Bee Farm for the year, me with my broad-brush, strategic macro-thinking, Duncan with his strange capacity for mending little bits of equipment that were already beyond redemption.

'I saw John last week,' announced Duncan, 'and he had something quite interesting to say.'

We had finished our basic maintenance tasks and were poring over last year's auction catalogue to identify early on the kind of things that we might want to buy this time around. For Duncan, the sight and feel of a catalogue was like cheap pornography to a sixteen-year-old boy, and I could always detect a spring in his step when he was working himself towards a decision to buy something from it. We were only a couple of weeks away from the arrival of Viktor's next nuc, and had therefore brought the Remain hive up to as perfect condition as we could to welcome its new tenants. We had replaced a rotten queen excluder with so many holes in it that it couldn't have excluded a medium-sized dog. We'd checked the Brexit hive for food, and given them some soft fondant as an Easter treat; we'd done a bit of Varroa treatment and got our hive records up to date. For a real beekeeper, this latter job would have entailed great swathes of writing about screened bottoms, propped covers, orientation flights, hive scent and dead bees on the porch. It would involve 30 different variables, from mites to queen cells and deformed wings; when complete, it would have provided a forensic log of our activity and the bees' condition, week after week, month after month. As it was, our log sheet just said: 'Welcome to the new season! Get foraging.'

I asked Duncan about John, who was our cricket club's treasurer and its most reliable batsman. An accountant by trade, he liked precision in his life, whether it was in the execution of a cover drive or the careful management of his smallholding at the foot of the Downs. He was also another, more experienced, beekeeper, and it was about this aspect of his life that Duncan had been talking to him.

'He got stung last week, and ended up in hospital.'

'You're joking,' I said. 'He's been doing this for years. He must have been stung by shed-loads of them.'

'Just the one this time. But he was having real trouble breathing afterwards, and eventually took himself off to hospital for a jab. Bit of a bastard, eh?' He looked suspiciously cheerful for someone who had just told a story about a friend in trouble.

'Terrible,' I said, tutting happily. 'Shall we give him a call?'

There are two inalienable truths in respect of beekeeping and stinging. The first is that you will get stung many times, however much you protect yourself, and you had better get used to it. The second is that if you start to experience a severe anaphylactic reaction after a sting, you need to stop the hobby. No ifs. No buts. Just stop. About five people die every year in Britain from bee, wasp and hornet stings[1] and, while a small number, it's also a good one not to be adding to. The way we looked at it, there was every chance that our number three batsman was now an ex-beekeeper and, if he wasn't, that Duncan and I could persuade him of the appalling risks he was letting himself in for by continuing. After all, retired beekeepers have no need of all that equipment and should be happy to see it go to a good home, rather than cluttering up the place. I made a mental note to emphasise this to John at the cricket nets the following week.

'You're too precious to the club,' we would say solicitously. 'And, by the way, are you doing anything with that newish National with the three supers I saw round your way last year?'

Along with honey, the sting is the factor most associated with bees by laymen. The first question that a neighbour will ask – understandably – when you begin to keep bees is along the lines of whether they are going to get stung.

There are two fundamental problems with being stung. First, it hurts (though plainly not as much as it hurts the bee, whose abdomen is routinely, and fatally, ripped out as she flies off). Secondly, it releases a pheromone that encourages other local bees to come over and have a go themselves, which is one of the reasons that it is always a good idea to remove the sting quickly, a job that can be done by enthusiastically rubbing the flat of the hive tool across the area of the sting. The bee only attacks as a means of defending her colony, her queen and, above all, her honey. She has a barbed stinger, modified by evolution from an old egg depositor, and this acts as a conduit that takes venom from the poison sac above. The venom contains a mixture of proteins that cause local inflammation and act as anti-coagulants, and its reaction varies among the people who get stung. A small percentage develop an anaphylactic reaction that presents as difficulty in breathing, swelling of the tongue and throat, and a weak, rapid pulse. If it all gets out of hand, you need adrenalin to sort out the problem – and unfortunately none of us knows from one year to the next if our own card will be marked the following season. In my own case, I can feel a sense of masochistic satisfaction when I survive the first sting of the season, as it indicates to me that I can continue safely for another year.

In a not very long list, the best thing about being stung by bees is that your body also receives a dose of hormones which many* believe acts as a powerful, if temporary, anti-arthritic treatment. I am not usually at the forefront of medical research, but I am able to testify to the efficacy of bee stings in this department. Because the jeans I wear to do my beekeeping have holes in the knees, I always get stung on the knees; and because my knees have crumbled after years of doing silly things with them in the army, I know when they have good days and bad days. And each time I am stung,

....

* Though clearly not the mainstream drug industry. Obviously.

I have a week of complete local pain relief in my knees. The only time that I was stung simultaneously on both knees, the pain disappeared completely.

Which is why, before you ask, I have never bothered to buy new trousers. I know the drill, the bees know the drill and, for a week, I walk happily.

Weeks passed, and the nuc from Viktor duly arrived on the doorstep.

'Any advice?' I asked, when I called to notify him of its safe arrival. We had dimly alluded to the starvation, after all, when we placed the order, as it seemed to us that his advice was a bigger plus than the potential minus of his disapproval.

'Don't mess it up this time,' he said. 'Be a good beekeeper. Think Ukrainian.'

So we thought Ukrainian. We homed our new colony in the vacant Remain hive, and left them for a few days to see how they adapted. Slowly, was the answer, but the effect that their arrival seemed to have on the Brexit hive a yard away to the west was impressive. Maybe it was just the rhythms of nature again, or maybe some dark competitive force had stirred in the depths of the brood box, but the work rate doubled, and then doubled again. What had been a relatively quiet landing board, one where a family of bees could have had an unhurried picnic, had turned into Heathrow in miniature. The small opening was crowded with bees crawling over each other to get out or in, as the residents of Brexit subconsciously seized their chance to get at the local delicacies before others did.

There is a tide in the affairs of men which, taken at the flood and all that, leads to great things. In this case, the arrival of the basis of the new Remain colony emboldened me to call John and solicitously ask after his recent anaphylaxis.

'You poor thing,' I said, as sympathetically as a man can when he is likely to benefit personally from the problem he is talking about. 'That must have been really horrible for you. I mean ending up in casualty after being stung.'

'Ah, I see,' he said. 'You want to know if I'm getting rid of any equipment.'

'The idea hadn't occurred to me. But I can see that you wouldn't want to go on after that sort of warning shot. And if you do eventually end up getting rid of any kit, give me a shout and I'll see what I can do for you.'

'I've got a crappy old National with a weak colony in it. You can come and get it when you want. But you're not getting any of the newer hives or the equipment till I'm dragged from here feet first.'

'I'll be over in twenty minutes.' I hung up and called Duncan.

'We're in business. We are officially up to three colonies as from tonight.'

Reflecting on our day's work when we had returned from John's house and sited the third hive at a discreet distance from the other two, we congratulated ourselves on increasing the number of hives by 200%, even if 66% of them were weak and problematic colonies and the remainder was an unproven nucleus from our friend in Oxfordshire.

Duncan's initial reaction, as always, was to go on to the Paynes website and see if this state of affairs provided the opportunity to spend ridiculous amounts of money on a fresh and completely useless piece of kit. Mine was to think of a witty and amusing name for the third colony.

'We have Brexit. We have Remain. What's the next logical name?'

We considered Trump Towers, but felt on balance it would depress us once the initial originality had worn off. We considered plays on the words 'Putin' and 'Kim Jong-un', but they were weak, even to us. So we thought back to the origins of the colony, and how we could honour its former owner. And thus the John Banks Memorial Hive was christened.

Looked at one way, we had three hives and were starting to get seriously into the business. Looked at another, we had two weak colonies and one unproven one, and we could as easily end up with none by the end of the season as three. In the year that we had worked together on the project, our initial capacity for self-deception had been replaced by a more British gloomy expectation of reality. What we needed to do was think radically, and accelerate nature to our own purposes. And one of the most obvious options was to merge the two weaker colonies into one strong one. It was the kind of thing our bearded YouTube farmer back in Alabama probably did four times before breakfast, but for us it was like converting base metal into gold. In nature, as in most things in life, less is more.

'Let's assume that Viktor's bees are as good as they always are,' said Duncan, 'and we just let them get on with it. Let's then assume that the Brexit queen is stronger than the Memorial one, and that only one of the colonies is really likely to work. Why don't we merge those two colonies and get one strong one?'

Duncan's flight of fancy seemed sensible, although merging two weak hives was something more normally done in the autumn, so that they were all raring to go by the beginning of the following season. Also, in the catalogue of our beekeeping activities this was by far the most grown-up thing we had ever considered, and we would ratchet ourselves up by one whole division if we could do it successfully. It was Premier League stuff, from decidedly lower-division players. It would be the kind of thing that we could drone on about in the pub ever after, just to demonstrate our countrymen credentials, and for a second I thought of Mr Fowler and wondered whether he had ever done something as technical as this.

'Do we kill one of the queens, or let them fight it out? And, if we do kill a queen, which one is it?'

Duncan got his phone out and Googled 'merging two bee colonies'.

'It says that the risk of leaving them to fight it out is that the winner is quite often badly injured and weakened by the fight, and isn't up to much. So I think we take out the Memorial queen.'

We both admitted later that this decision was motivated partly by us not being psychologically capable of getting rid of Theresa after all we had been through with her, and she with us. Not for the first time, she had dodged a bullet. It took a quarter of an hour to locate the Memorial queen, but no more than twenty seconds to dispatch her, albeit making her in the process the first bee in our charge that we had ever knowingly harmed. It seemed a strange and counter-intuitive activity to be sure, but it clearly one that is familiar to bee-keepers up and down the land.

The next afternoon, we started by cleaning the bottom of the frames in the Memorial hive in order that the bees didn't start making what is called brace comb off them, and thus rendering the next part of the exercise futile. Then we placed the allegedly stronger Brexit brood box below the allegedly weaker Memorial one, and separated them with a sheet of newspaper, as we had planned to do with Brexit and Remain the previous autumn. Do it like this, the textbooks suggested, and they will be greeting each other like old friends once contact is established. Do it any quicker, and you will have the fight to end all fights on your hands. While we were aware that the Brexit bees probably preferred the *Daily Mail* or *The Sun*, the only paper we had to hand was a *Sunday Times*, and the sheet we chose was a full-length feature on gender reassignment from the previous weekend's edition. It was either that or an article on ISAs from the financial pages, and we didn't think either colony was up to digesting that.*

All we needed to do now was go away for a couple of days and see what had happened when we got back. The signal that the process was effectively complete would be the presence of bits of chewed-up newspaper around the entrance.

Mr Fowler used to say that the time to plant potatoes was when the soil was warm enough to sit on comfortably with your bare backside. Whether he ever did this himself is a mystery, but I still like to think of the half-shocked, half-delighted Mrs Fowler looking out of the kitchen window at her husband perched out there among the spring greens, testing the temperature in the traditional way with a far-away look in his eye. Sometimes those days come in mid-March, and sometimes you have to wait until early April, but there is

---

* Duncan was a *Sunday Sport* man at heart, but even he baulked at the idea of giving the bees a front cover with the giant headline 'Boris Sex Dwarf Drowns in Giant Trifle'. Even bees have limits.

always one particular day when winter concedes the ground to spring and the world outside is suddenly alive with vivid green and with expectation.

That harbinger of summer himself, the first swallow, was flitting about in the paddock on the sunlit morning two days later when I went down to measure the success of our operation, and I found myself wondering how many times he had made that long journey from West Africa to be with us. And how many of our bees he would eat by the time the summer was done and he was heading off once more to brave the hawks, falcons, owls, gulls and Maltese gunmen and netters between him and his winter feeding grounds.

Gingerly, noting the tell-tale signs of newspaper fragments, I opened the top of the Memorial hive. Having grown used to doing the technical side of beekeeping by the seat of our pants, and tending to get the results that we deserved, I was surprised to see an air of orderly calm in the Memorial brood box, and orderly calm below at the doorway of Brexit. Bees were going about their business in the purposeful way they were supposed to, the way the book told us they should, and for a second my Sagittarian brain was imagining the serried ranks of hives that must surely follow as we grew the Upperfold Bee Farm to its full potential.

I was awoken from the reverie by a sharp pain in my hand as an incoming bee stung me for no particular reason. I gloved up and swapped the frames around so that the ones with brood were down at the bottom, and the ones without were at the top. I hadn't got to the bit in the book about what happened next, but I already had the quiet satisfaction of knowing that our first tiny foray into genetic engineering had gone spectacularly well. Tomorrow would come soon enough.

Our enterprise had survived the winter, and summer beckoned somewhere out there over the southern horizon. As the sun climbed a little more in the sky with each lengthening day, and as the damson tree above the hives blossomed into its pure white, I felt a tiny shock of pure elation at the approaching season. Seeing and smelling and hearing the signs of the coming bounty felt, as it always feels, like a renewal of life itself.

If last year was the summer of trial and tragedy, I thought, the coming one would be full of hope and honey.

Chapter 10

THE KEBAB VAN

May

....

In winter, I plot and plan.
In spring I move.
HENRY ROLLINS

....

A few days after the Feast of Saint George, Duncan went over to the dark side.

Hitherto, ours had been an entrepreneurial exercise, buccaneering even, one whose basic structure was punctuated by rule breaks and subversiveness. Belonging to nothing, and answerable to no one, our progress came as the result of a creative tension between Duncan's profligate attention to detail and my own tight-fisted big-picture strategising. To be fair, we learned from our many mistakes, and were no longer a liability around *Apis mellifera*; our second season promised liquid gold in quantities about which we had previously not dared to dream.

I could see there was an issue when Duncan walked across the gravel of our driveway for our weekly hive inspection that Saturday morning.

'How's your week been?' I asked.

'Fine, mate. Yours?' And on we went in this vein for a minute or two before he came out with it.

'Sorry I didn't ask you, mate, but I signed on to the Defra database last night, and registered our colonies.' I assumed he was joking. Defra* was part of big government, and big government was the enemy of enterprise. It had the smack of irritating people in suits, which was very much what we had been trying to get away from.

'Course you have,' I laughed.

'No, really. I kept getting told that we should have registered our bees by now, and that we would get into trouble if the authorities found out about it before we told them.'

'They're insects, Duncan, not livestock. They come and go as they please. The last thing we need is Big Brother poking his nose in while we're struggling to learn it all. Anyway, what kind of trouble could we get into? I mean, really.'

This was as close to a disagreement as we had come in our fourteen months of working together, and cross though I

....

* Department for Environment, Food and Rural Affairs.

might have been, part of me actually felt rather honoured that he had taken control and made a decision above my head. It started to tilt the balance of leadership his way, which was no bad thing. Emboldened by my quiet reaction, he took a print-out of the paperwork from his pocket.

'Look,' he said proudly. 'We've got a unique NBU* number, a link to the Bee Base and a contact number for our very own regional bee inspector.' His innocent pleasure reminded me of a moment half a century before when I had got my membership card and badge for the Ian Allan Locospotters Club, where the simple fact of my having a personal serial number meant that for the first time I amounted to more than just being the son of my father. To have joined what I now accept was a rather esoteric grouping of people who derived pleasure from seeing numbered trains passing routinely through stations was akin to planting a flag on the foothills of manhood. Duncan would have still been a dozen years away from inflicting himself on an unsuspecting world at that point.

I had to admit that it all looked refreshingly unauthoritarian, thanking us as it did for signing up and offering us lots of help and advice, plus a Pest and Disease Inspection Programme. We went indoors and logged in to the Bee Base, and via that to the fourteen-page Healthy Bee Plan.

....

* National Bee Unit.

'So long as they don't call me a "stakeholder", I'll live with it,' I said, but they had done so by the third line of the first paragraph, and so lost me for ever.

Our Saturday morning inspections were not just an opportunity to have a beer before opening time, but a necessary routine to ensure that the two colonies weren't getting up to stuff. And the 'stuff' we didn't want them to get up to was the creation of additional queen cells that would lead to a new queen on the block and the uncontrolled swarming that followed on from that.

Colonies should be inspected with a maximum interval of ten days at this time of year. More than that, and the workers have the time in between to create and feed a queen cell to the point that she is just about to hatch, which is normally the trigger point for the old queen to move half her colleagues out for alternative accommodation. More frequent checks than that just slow down the honey production, not least because the calming smoke that accompanies the inspection also causes the residents to feed themselves up in preparation of an expected long journey, and so depletes the stores.

There are two types of queen cell, namely good ones and bad ones. 'Good' ones, which tend to hang off a vertical bit of the frame, are a sign that the colony is thriving and knows that it will soon run out of room. The workers start to create a new queen so that the old one, once success is assured, can lead out half the bees to create a new colony, and thus achieve reproduction: great if you are bee, not so good if you are a beekeeper. A 'bad' queen cell is created when there is something wrong with the existing queen, and the workers are planning for supersedure; these tend to be located in the thick of the frame in a deliberate attempt to hide the activity from the ailing queen, whose first instinct would be to come over and kill the potential rival.

'What's that over there?' you can imagine her saying.

'Oh that,' they might reply. 'Nothing. I think it's just some sort of an art installation. Nice, isn't it?' And they would whistle thoughtfully until she was clear of the area.

The best thing to do with a bad cell is ignore it and allow nature to take its assertive course. Paradoxically, the good cells are more of a problem for the beekeeper than the bad.

Skilled beekeepers thus have a list of options they can follow once they have identified good queen cells, ranging from simply twisting them off the frame and throwing them away (which will often achieve little or nothing, possibly even accelerating the inevitable swarm), to getting rid of all but a couple so as to leave an heir and a spare, or artificially swarming the colony. This last is deep into the realms of grown-up bee husbandry.

On this particular Saturday, we had other things to worry about once we had ensured that our girls weren't about to bunk off any time soon into a tree in the adjacent park. Over the previous few evenings, I had noticed that the pollen-carrying panniers on the back legs of the returning foragers were bright yellow, a sure sign that they had located the fields of oilseed rape (or OSR, as we call it in the business) a mile or so to the east of our garden.

Too much is never enough for a foraging bee and oilseed rape. It attracts them over to its fields like a kebab van to an undergraduate after a night on the lash, and it calls across the miles for them to return again and again until the last yellow flower has died back and the field normalised. Again, this is great for the bee, but problematical for the beekeeper, in that OSR honey crystallises very rapidly on the frames in the supers and quickly makes it impossible to extract. Once the bees have capped it over, it would be easier to explain the velocity of money supply to my Jack Russell than to extract it into pots for future consumption.

'Are you thinking what I'm thinking?' asked Duncan. Given that what Duncan was normally thinking about was Norwich's relegation woes, or ways of spending hard-earned cash we hadn't got on equipment we didn't need, I told him that it was unlikely.

'We take a crop now. Get honey in the bank before the season has even really started.'

I saw his point. This year's honey in the larder would be an insurance policy against later failure, and would silence the doubters like Jim. We agreed that we should leave it for another couple of weeks, and then remove it, but only from the stronger, Remain, hive. Brexit had enough issues settling down to its merged colonies for us to risk further exacerbating things by removing their honey.

Pleased with our morning's work, we repaired to the terrace to trial a new and local craft lager and start talking some serious economics to the dog.

Two weekends on, late spring had arrived in waves of warmth and bright green from the valley floor below. For a few short weeks, everything had an urgency to it, the secret burden bestowed by the brief seasons allocated by nature.

I stood on the lawn in the weak early morning sunshine, feeling the almost physical change rising up my body from the dew on the grass, knowing more than ever that we only get one go at life, one shot at being who we need to be. In my other life of trains, airports, showrooms and offices, the seasons were simply what arbitrarily marked out buying periods and trade shows. They were a function of dates on a calendar, and not the beating of tiny hearts.

I might have expected to have been changed in some way by my bees, but not like this: the £1,000 or so that we had spent on the supporting equipment and activities was going to be dwarfed by the real cost in the decline of my future earnings, but deep down, I knew that there was no going back. I realised that I was levering myself off the career hamster-wheel a decade earlier than most people. In some ways it felt like I was playing truant from school, and that it would only be a matter of time before my parents received the call from the head teacher that would summon me back to my studies. At the same time, when the sun shone on my back, and when the words started to flow like the honey I wanted to write about, I knew for certain that I had bowed inelegantly out of the rat race once and for all. This particular rat was starting to develop alternative plans.

Back in some childhood memory of half a century ago, I saw Mr Fowler's early potatoes earthed up and swelling in his immaculate vegetable patch. Here in the reality of the present, though, I had to make do with Duncan coming round the corner of the house in a Norwich City strip.

'I've been thinking,' he said as he put his clobber down on the kitchen table. 'We could do with a queen-marking set. And possibly some more foundation sheets for the supers. So I've put an order in.' Duncan, I sometimes felt, had the single-handed ability to nudge national economies out of recession. Greece should have borrowed him for a week or two in 2010; they might have saved much heartache.

Cheerfully, we prepared ourselves for spinning out the frames of oilseed rape honey. Down from the loft came the enormous spinner; out from the cupboard came the old sieve, and up from the cellar came the jars for sterilising. I mentioned to Duncan that this somehow felt as if it was disturbing the natural pulse of things, helping ourselves to the benefit of work we didn't feel we had done yet.

'Crap,' he said. 'Have you been drinking? It's their job.'
'You wouldn't make much of a vegan,' I told him.

The pleasure of gathering our second harvest of honey was still intense, even if it was less life-changing than the previous summer's episode. Whereas that had been pioneering stuff carried out in a festival atmosphere, it was now almost routine. Where there had been only seven pots, now we were the proud possessors of 27. We were no longer savages being shown a simple conjuring trick by visitors from an alien world, we were just men getting on with a job of work. We had decanted about 23 jars when my phone went. It was Jim.

'I've got another swarm,' he told me. 'Almost on the same tree. Do you want it?'

I looked at Duncan and knew in an instant that this was our chance to get the third colony up and running, and thereby fill up the John Banks Memorial Hive. There would be other swarms, but there was no guarantee that we would find out about them until rival beekeepers had heard on the grapevine and got there first. After all, there is little more annoying than the sight of a rival beekeeper competently dumping a fresh colony into his cardboard wine box. Besides, this one would cost us no more than the diesel it would take to get the five miles to Jim's field and back, rather than the £150 needed to buy a decent fresh nuc. We accelerated the decanting of the last few jars of thick, light-coloured oilseed rape honey, made our apologies to Caroline for the mess, then dived into the pickup to make the short journey to Midhurst to take the swarm.

Jim was sceptical when we got there, but he had to admit that the Upperfold bee enterprise had evolved a long way since that wet Sunday two years ago when I had cut his damp swarm away from the branch they were on. Gone was the tatty old 1960s equipment that Jim had lent me, replaced by the results of Duncan's many night-time forays onto the Paynes website. We looked the part and, what was more, we acted it. Despite the fact that Duncan had never taken a swarm, the two of us took no more than ten minutes to get it into our box, wrap it up in an old blue dust sheet and put it on the ground while Jim made us a coffee.

'You'll be registering your hives with Defra next,' he said, as we climbed back into the pickup to speed back to the headquarters of our growing empire.

'Did you tell him about Defra?' Duncan asked me once we were on our way.

'No,' I said after a short pause. 'What Jim really hates, deep down, is incompetence. That comment was as close to praise as you are ever likely to get with him.'

'Rehiving' the swarm, and thus turning it into a productive colony, is an ostensibly simple job that is easy to get wrong, particularly if your name is Duncan, or Roger. Having tried and failed with the 'walking in' technique with the white sheet all those months ago, we decided to go for the 'dumping it straight in' approach this time round, which just consisted of taking the lid off the empty hive and moving a few frames out so that there was room for the swarm to be dropped in. Once done, there are a number of things that the beekeeper still doesn't know, principally whether he has a virgin queen on his hands (in which case she will need to go on her mating flight), and whether the new colony is free of disease. Our new friends at the National Bee Unit recommended on their website that we considered setting up an isolation hive for a few weeks, but the concept was so far out of our knowledge base that, in the end, we just shoved them in, put the lid back on and waited to see what would happen.

Besides, we had left one hell of a mess in the kitchen.

Throughout May, the Saturday mornings should have continued to the beat of the same drum as before, and they would have done were it not for the 'C' word.

It was cricket, after all, that had brought Duncan and me together in the first place,[1] and May was the month when we would first drag our bodies back onto the various fields of dreams where we tried to amount to something heroic. 'You can always find a distraction if you're looking for one,' said US golfer Tom Kite, and he was right. The British summer was absolutely stuffed full of them, red hot ways of spending your time, and every single one of them the enemy of good beekeeping. And the particular problem with our brand of social cricket was that the matches were normally played on a Saturday, the very day that we had always allocated to checking our hives. Some deep childish instinct parked in a lay-by in my ageing body persuaded me that this would be fine, and that because we had done all the hard yards in the early season, the bees would basically do what they were supposed to.

As it turned out, they didn't, but they were kind enough to give us fair warning.

As one of the cricket side's two skippers, I normally tried to manipulate the batting order so that Duncan and I had a partnership. That way we could continue our bee conversations at sporadic intervals during the afternoon and thus convince ourselves that we were being conscientious. And, because he tended to keep wicket, I would place myself at first slip so that the intervals between balls and overs could be punctuated with talk of brood capping, bee space and burr comb. It must have come over to visiting batsmen as a curious form of sledging, but it worked for us.

It was during one of these matches, one afternoon on a ground some 30 miles away, that I noticed as I was padding up that my phone had about six missed calls from Caroline. One missed call normally meant 'could I collect milk on the way home', but six could only be bad news. With a sense of foreboding, I dialled up the message:

'I'm looking at your new scruffy hive,' she said in a measured way, 'and all I can see is a coating of bees on its front wall, and a load of them flying in circles around it. It doesn't look good.'

It meant only one thing; our new swarm had swarmed again, the little bastards. She offered to put on a veil and try to take the swarm if I explained over the phone how to do it. For a second I was inclined to take her up on the offer, which was above and beyond any normal call of marital duty, but a tiny, protective bit of me didn't want to put her in the firing line.

'That's really sweet of you,' I said. 'But don't worry. It looks like we've got a bunch of career swarmers so they'll probably just head off again even if you do round them up. I'll sort them when I get home if they're still there.' But deep down my heart was singing: a volunteer is worth twenty pressed men, and Caroline's willingness to join in augured well for the coming months and years.

I joined Duncan in the middle and gave him the bad tidings from over the county boundary.

'Damn,' he said. 'What did they want to go and do that for?'

It was the second innings of the match, so theoretically we were free to go as soon as we had both completed our individual contributions.

'We might just save the situation if we get home quickly enough,' I said. The well-being of the team was one thing, but the diminution of our apiary by 33% was quite another. Oftentimes, bees would hang around for a few hours once they had swarmed, so all was not yet entirely lost. 'Just hit everything, and we're bound to get out quickly.'

I was a fragile batsman at best, so the prospect of getting out quickly was not a difficult one to imagine, or an unlikely one for me to deliver. Nor, once I had returned to the pavilion, would anyone suspect anything more than my usual diet of strange shot selections washed down by the warm beer of ineptitude.

It didn't work out like that. The sporting gods, who so often saw fit to decant me back into my car on the back of yet another disappointing performance, decided that today was the day when I would hit everything off the middle of the bat, and miss nothing. Thirty years of praying to those same sporting gods to give me a break, and they decided to do so on a day when I really didn't want one. My first stroke, a gigantic and ugly heave off my toes, was still going upwards when it cleared the trees on the boundary edge; other shots followed in the same vein, and Duncan was doing the same thing, to the same effect. After about half an hour, Duncan was clean bowled, but not before we had put on 60 between us, and still I couldn't get out. I could see him pacing up and down on the boundary, jangling his car keys with impatience, but it made no difference. Each time the bowler went back to his mark, all I could think of were the scouts from that bee colony flying back to the group and saying: 'Listen in, girls.

We've found a great tree to go and live in. And do you know what? It's 80 foot up.'

When we won the match, I was still there on 47 not out, my highest score for years. My co-skipper wandered out with a celebratory cold can of lager for me, and would brook no argument about me heading off before I had drunk it.

'Man of the match,' he said with finality. 'You can't just disappear.'

An hour and a half later, we arrived home having challenged every speed limit in the county, went straight down to the John Banks Memorial Hive and found, predictably enough, nothing. A few wasps were flying around the landing board in a desultory way, but of bees there were none. Many beekeepers clip one or both wings of their queens so that they can't go far in these circumstances, but we hadn't yet done that as we didn't even know if she had completed her mating flight.

We never saw them again, but we were truly grateful that the idea hadn't caught on with the other two colonies. It was a lesson well learned, even if for the second time of asking, and the great thing was that Jim need never know.

Even with the loss of that colony, we ended May ahead of where we had started it.

Remain and Brexit, in their different ways, were thriving hives, their populations multiplying quickly in the late spring warmth. Sure, we had lost a colony to swarming, but it was a colony that we hadn't paid for, hadn't had a fortnight before, and that therefore didn't need to appear on the balance sheet. With 27 pots of oilseed rape honey safely tucked away in storage, we had something to show for the season before it had even really started, meaning that anything else we achieved was almost a bonus.

Away from the hive, I was finally arriving at a settled view of what I wanted to do with the next bit of my life. And while the bees couldn't take any direct credit for what was going on in my brain, there was no doubt that a season of watching them working with the grain of nature, rather than against it, had pushed me into what passed for a similar pattern of behaviour.

Simply, I wanted to do what I loved as well as I possibly could. To wake up each morning, Mondays included, just aching to get out there doing stuff. To ensure that the footprints I left behind were useful ones. To make people laugh. To drink lots of whisky. And, in order to do all that, I needed to be spending my time writing about stuff.

And, on top of everything, my season's batting average had climbed from 7.5 to 20.7.

Things were looking up.

Chapter 11

THE PIPER AT THE GATES OF DAWN

June

....

*The keeping of bees ... is like
directing the sunbeams.*
HENRY DAVID THOREAU

....

It was early on a Saturday morning, and I was sitting at the table on my terrace, cradling a mug of tea between my hands, quietly allowing the coming day's business to suggest and arrange itself in my head. There were things that always needed doing about the place, and early on a weekend morning was a good time to start. The midsummer sun was already long up in the south-east, even if no one else was, and there were the faint beginnings of warmth in the paving slabs under my feet. A buzzard mewed out over the park, and I watched him soar on the day's first thermals, possibly looking for a pigeon late to leave its roost, or a rabbit kit that had strayed too far from its burrow. His constant presence has enriched us for years, but he has seen off the little kestrels who used to spend the summer here. But then that's the inconvenient thing about nature that people tend to forget: much of it is a zero-sum game. Buzzards up, kestrels down; badgers up, hedgehogs down; seals up, salmon down.

I wasn't thinking about bees this morning, not consciously anyway, but I started to notice one hovering at a dandelion on the unmown piece of lawn nearest me. I began to piece together in my mind exactly what she might be doing, and to dovetail her day to mine so that we were more nearly breathers of the same air and players in the same theatre.

On a whim, I called her Greta, and I decided that she was one of mine.

That dandelion is Greta's first stopping point since leaving the hive 70 yards away.

She was born, which is to say that she emerged from her brood cell, on the last day of April, and she will die towards the end of tomorrow. Around 600 million generations have gone before her since her species evolved more or less into what it is now and, in many senses, she is older than civilisation itself.

She is driven only by the one imperative of her own contribution to helping the colony survive and thrive, having no capacity to think independently of her own welfare or plans. Her role is simply to provide nectar, pollen and water from the world outside and to have it taken off her when she returns to the colony. Like humans, she has the privilege of thought, but only in terms of which signs lead to things that are sweet, and which don't. Hers is a loveless, brutally practical world, with no concept of tiredness or time, other than the relentless call of the available hours of daylight.

About a minute ago, she crawled her way across and around the brood frames to the little exit hole of the hive, stood for a brief while on the landing board to get her bearings, and then flew. She flies at about fifteen miles per hour on wings that beat 200 times a second, backwards and forwards rather than up and down, so that she creates both forward motion and a vortex of low pressure around her for easier lift. Generally, she flies in a straight line. From the instant she is airborne, she is summoned to specific flowers by their colours, but also by their electric fields: she never plans to go to that dandelion first, or to any other particular flower on her foraging trip for that matter. The dandelion is calling *her*. The same positive electric fields tell her whether specific flowers have been visited recently by other bees and therefore risk being temporarily short of nectar. This prevents her from wasting precious energy. And, because she can see in ultraviolet, she sees the dandelion not as a monochrome image, but as rich and luminous in the centre, so she knows exactly where on the flower to direct her attentions.[1]

When Greta reaches the dandelion, the negative charge around its petals reacts with the positive charge around Greta, and some of the pollen literally jumps up off the petal towards her, meaning in a strange way that the flower is flying to the bee as surely as the bee is flying to the flower. The orange-red pollen attaches itself to the panniers on her back legs without her ever knowing it.

But pollen is not even half the story of why she is on that flower: she needs its nectar. Nectar is really no more than the reward that the plant gives her for her cross-pollinating services, but it is the key constituent of the honey she is contributing to, and which some deep instinct tells her will sustain the colony for the coming winter, long after she is dead and gone. Once she lands on the flower, she deploys her proboscis to where the nectar is stored, and sucks it out like a child sucks a drink through a straw. She will drink it in until she has extracted all that is in her reach, possibly a milligram, and store it in her second stomach before lifting back up into the summer sky and moving to the next source. She is no fool; if she is in a patch of flowers that are rich in nectar she will stay in the immediate area and feed on maybe 30 or 40 before flying back to the hive. Equally, when times are leaner, she will fly as far as she needs, possibly a return journey of five miles in all, to collect the same amount.

She is lucky with that dandelion, as she has been with this particular summer, for this is mid-June when there is often a dangerous interval – beekeepers call it the 'June gap' – between the bounty of the hedgerow blossoms in April and May and the coming summer rush of flowers in July. June is consequently a potentially tricky time of year for the colony, where starvation can ambush them almost overnight. The spring and early summer have been kind this year, though, and there is just about enough to go around. And she is lucky that we don't use herbicide weedkillers round here, because if we did, that dandelion would likely kill her by quickly stripping away the beneficial bacteria from her gut and leaving her susceptible to every infection going. Greta is blissfully unaware that she is competing with millions of other foragers in the same small area, from feral honeybee hives to bumblebees and from wasps to moths and butterflies. It is the genius of nature to be able to satisfy them all, and sometimes it is the genius of man to deny every one of them.

She will need water, as well, even though she doesn't like to get her feet wet. She will be aware of the local water sources, from ponds to leaky hoses, and instinct tells her when the water is needed back in the hive for a number of reasons, but especially to feed its temperature control system in the summer.* Only about 30% of the colony's population forages, so in a way she is constantly doing what she does for another two bees. But that still means there are around 15,000 bees from her hive out on the forage this morning, maybe translating into a quarter of a million journeys, and ten million individual visits to flowers. It is small wonder that the production of honey in her hive starts to accelerate rapidly once the June gap is done and high summer is in full swing: sometimes it only takes a few days to fill a new super with honey when the pickings are rich. With bees like Greta, everything is about scale. In the heights of summer, about 30,000 workers will be making up to a dozen flights a day each from that hive, and the stores build quickly.

Using the sun as a directional marker, she eventually returns to the hive, for an instant more powerful than the stepsisters she has left inside it. For as she flies through the air, she collides with millions of charged particles, from dust downwards, which combine to tear electrons away from her outer shell, leaving her ten times more electrically charged than she was when she left. This means that, as she dances her waggle dance on the vertical surface of the comb,

....

* Hive temperature is of vital importance to the colony and is precisely controlled. The temperature of the brood chamber is held at around 32°C so that the brood develops normally. When it's too hot, bees ventilate by fanning the warm air away from the nest, or by evaporating water. When it's too cold, they generate heat by flexing their flight muscles.

she can move her neighbours around without even making contact. As their antennae approach her, they are repelled, and this gives her the space to make her point, and her point is to inform the others where her food source is.

This is her last full day alive, before the hard work ultimately kills her, and she still has much to do. She is not aware that her body is starting to fail her, that her wings are beginning to shred. All she knows as she sets off for the next of her dozen or so foraging flights is that she must do this until nightfall makes it impossible to carry on. Once back in the hive, she will pass on the nectar in her stomach by regurgitating the liquid into another bee's mouth, a process that may get repeated five or six times before the final worker in the process adds what is now the honey into an available cell. At this point the honey is still liquid, too liquid, in fact, for it to remain in the cell by its own devices; so other bees will fan it dry with their wings to speed up the process of evaporation. From the time Greta was on that dandelion by my terrace to the honey being in the cell in the frame might be anywhere between an hour and half a day.

Back she will come from her last flight of the midsummer day. Same buzzard in the same sky above her, same pigeon in the same roost, same rabbit litter on the same bit of grass near the hive. For a moment, she stands on the landing board just as she did fourteen hours ago, only this time she folds her wings back and bundles her tired body through the small opening, one of a hundred or so bees in this short minute of day-ending forage. Past the guards she crawls, past the nurses on the outer parts of the frame, maybe even past her queen, until she disgorges the final bounty of the day into the waiting mouth of another bee, and she can rest. Even then, she will be keenly attuned to the prevailing beat of the pheromones in her hive, until she finally settles into the circadian rhythm of maybe five hours of sleep, until tomorrow comes.

And tomorrow will come early to the hive. Sunrise will be at 4.45, and the bees will be close behind it. They know that the dry spell will be over for a day or two after that, and that rain is in the air. When it comes, the harvest will have to wait until it stops again, so everything is about making use of the day.

Greta's day is over, her life almost done. Twice as many bees are being born in the colony at the moment than are dying, and it will only be her great-great nieces who will get the benefit of her labours once the days have shortened and the frost is tumbling once again down the hill into the village.

These thoughts about Greta's theoretical day had moved through my mind in maybe a minute and a half, during which time my eyes followed her progress through the flowers on the edge of the lawn and ultimately over my neighbour's hedge and away from my view.

Unaccountably, I found I was missing her, or at least her direct presence in my life. Our heavily interconnected world gives precious few opportunities for simplicity, sometimes even when we actively seek them out. If we are not careful, one day, swamped in things we don't need, on which we have spent money that we don't have, we will realise that we have accidentally handed over the keys to our lives to a third party. To share a moment with a perfect relic of prehistory is sometimes to feel that you have beaten the machine, that you have snatched the keys back, even if just for that moment. I felt privileged beyond calculation.

I wandered out onto the grass in my bare feet, noticing a red-tailed bumblebee here on a little clover flower, a common carder bee there on a lone geranium. A year ago, I couldn't have told the difference between the two, or between any of the other pollinator species in my garden, but these were all now as much part of my new world as the honeybee. As with the honeybee, so with the others: I had started to immerse myself into their world. Years of abject failure in the sciences at school had burst out, many years later, into a new thirst for practical knowledge. It turned out that biology was a piece of cake for me if I was up to my elbows in 50,000 insects on a weekly basis. Anyone could be a biologist when the reward was honey.

Besides, how could I do my bit to help save them if I didn't understand what was harming them? How could I tell their story if I didn't even know where it started?

Around me, my secret day was metamorphosing into a shared one, and from now on it belonged not just to me. Somewhere down the village street a car door shut, and I counted the seconds until its engine fired and it left for its first errand of the day, its clamour gradually merging again with the silence. A squirrel ran the full length of the park wall from no specific place to somewhere else. More birds were active in the garden now; a small charm of goldfinches on the nijer seed feeder of our bird table, a fat thrush pecking at the lawn. Out in the park, a great spotted woodpecker thrummed its territorial hammering, and, in the distance, something that might have been a cuckoo, or might have been a sparrow-hawk, flew heavily between two high oaks. I leant against the fence and for an instant wondered why anyone ever left this place.

Momentarily, I also found myself thinking that far too much effort has been tied up in trying to rid ourselves of our sense of awe. In constantly trying to explain away the rainbow, we have overlooked its simple beauty; in constantly seeking to prove, or disprove, the existence of a higher power, we have lost the joy of uncertainty. Sometimes, the human spirit just needs to admit that it doesn't know, and doesn't care that it doesn't know: things are as they are because they are, and that is good. There were so many things that I still didn't understand, and the more I knew that, the more content I was, and the less completely I needed to understand. For a fraction of an instant on that early morning lawn, I knew that I was no more or less than Greta. The only thing that was important was that I was here, now, alone in the silence until the world came back and the spell was broken.

I heard a car pull up on the road outside and knew, at 5.45 in the morning, it had to be Duncan. He would be on his way home from a night of work in New Covent Garden, and would be coming to sit on the log by the hive for a while and be an interested spectator to the activity all around before the demands of his young family grew too loud to ignore. Like me, he saw our bees as a connection to the wider natural world around him, and, like me, he was moved by the richness and simplicity of it all. His arrival was unexpected, and at first I found myself relishing the prospect of sharing this tiny run of magic with him and his uncomplicated version of friendship. But in the same instant I knew that there are some moments in our lives that are made for sharing, and some we need to savour all alone. This one, today, was for solitude. For him, as it had been for me.

The log by the hive was a pew in the cathedral of the new day, and the birdsong all around its choral echo. To hear nature speak, you had first to create silence; to hear her sing, you had to open your heart. To be freed of the filaments that bind you, you had sometimes simply to ignore them. This was not a moment for small talk. It was a time for wonder.

Eyes gently stinging with the simple beauty of it all, I picked up my empty mug, slipped into the kitchen and left Duncan to the deepening blue of the new day.

Chapter 12

THE JACKPOT

August

....

We must give more in order to get more.
It is the generous giving of ourselves
that produces the generous harvest.
ORISON SWETT MARDEN

....

The long hot summer had made the nights still and air-less, and the thick walls of our old cottage had started to radiate heat, whatever the temperature outside. It was a time of fitful rest, and of early waking; of seeing the first pale glimmer of eastern light through the gaps in the curtain, and of dipping in and out of sleep like a swimmer in the surf, until the new day was already too warm to ignore. This was a time of day when the boundary between dreams and reality was at its narrowest, as each half-truth nestled up to its real-life equivalent and then rolled away again, leaving me wondering momentarily which was which.

Up in the tulip tree, a collared dove's three-tone calling became more insistent, and the last vestiges of sleep fell away. I lay still for a while, watching the developing brightness through the curtains, and listening to the process of the natural world getting about its daily business in the countryside beyond – the single call of a cock pheasant, the Canada Geese noisily flighting in to the lake in the park over the wall, a tractor going through its gears in a field beyond the village. But the sounds I could hear were also the signs of the season remorselessly moving towards autumn: that pheasant's plumage was brightening and his tail was lengthening for the winter ahead; those geese were fattening up for the hard times to come; that tractor was tedding a late cut of hay. Quite suddenly, I knew that this was the year when I could decide to move with it, or to fight against it as I always did, to look forward to the coming winter rather than mourn the passing summer. There had been moments like this many times in the previous couple of years, but this time around, the bees had slowly changed me.

I assessed by the changing rhythms of her breathing at what stage Caroline was in the waking process.

'You awake?' I whispered.

'No,' came a muffled voice from the pillow. I left it for a minute or two.

'I think I've finally decided to leave,' I said.

'Leave what?' It hadn't occurred to me that she might wonder exactly who or what it was that I was going to leave. Five minutes before, she had been fast asleep.

'Work.' I paused, waiting for a reaction. 'The only way I will ever do something different is if I have no option.'

'Do it,' she said.

'Really?'

'Really,' she replied. 'But let me go back to sleep first.'

Four hours later, I had handed in my notice to the company that I had worked for, and had loved, for over a quarter of a century. They deserved greater commitment, and I knew it. Equally, I had run out of road that allowed me to be professionally dissatisfied for any longer. I had no clear plan of what I was going to do, or how, far less how I was going to pay for it, but I knew that if I didn't do it now, I never would.

'Done it,' I texted Caroline later on.

'Done what?' she asked.

It had been the longest of long hot summers, and Britain had become an outdoor country for a while, a country of parched grass, picnics and cricket matches that never got rained off. People talked of global warming and water-saving measures, but for our bees it was a time of plenty. We had survived the swarming season with no more scares, and had marvelled at our own competence as we checked our hives each weekend. Frames in the brood box were bulging out with the sheer weight of the bees that were on them, and of the brood within the cells of the foundation; the neighbouring frames in the supers above them were heavy with honey. It was what the word 'cornucopia' had been coined for, I told Duncan one morning, but it was early in the day and he was hungover, and he told me to stop being a dick and using long words. Duncan had banned the use of long words in our partnership ever since I had called him out for describing the muted evening peal of church bells filtering up from the valley as 'sentiquintially' English.

For the first time, we added second levels of supers onto the hives, thus doubling our potential harvest, and we watched the bees remorselessly colonise the new wax foundation they found there. It was all so different to the early days of uncertainty, days when I would stand by the landing board of the brood box of our first hive in our first season, counting individual bees in as they returned from their foraging, and then text the results to Duncan. These days, each time we opened one of the crown boards to get inside a hive, we would be met by that ceaseless pulse of seemingly random mass movement that I had first seen when my young eyes had nervously peered into Mr Fowler's hive half a century before.

Duncan might have been nearly 25 years younger than me, but his reasoned and researched approach had eventually given him a claim to such leadership as ever existed in the

Upperfold Bee Farm. After being in charge of people all my adult life, I was content to follow, knowing that he was the adult thinking things through and I was the child blinking in wonder at it all and trying to get up to things without being caught. Over the last year and a half, our relationship had evolved from one that simply embraced the pure adventure of a new hobby, to one that, underneath the bravado and beer, strove for increasing competence, and that was determined not to kill off any more honeybees through our own stupidity.

'The language of friendship,' said Henry David Thoreau, 'is not words but meanings.'* Those hours spent staring at the entrance of one hive or another, watching the smoke circle up from Duncan's cheroot, were often close to silent, the unfolding action in front of us doing its own version of the talking.

Jim came up to visit unannounced one morning during one of those silences, ostensibly to drop off an invitation to something or other, but in reality to check us out.

'How's the colony you took from me in May getting on?'

'Really well, mate,' said Duncan, pointing down at the Brexit hive. The intensity and enthusiasm of his dishonesty took me by surprise for a minute. The inheritors of the swarm

....

* His own friend and fellow natural philosopher, Ralph Waldo Emerson, perhaps got even closer to the mark when he wrote that 'it is one of the blessings of old friends that you can afford to be stupid with them'.

we had taken from Jim's farm were, for all we knew, currently in residence two miles away high up in the crook of an oak tree, throwing debauched parties and creating artisan blends of wild comb honey. Wherever else they were, it was manifestly not where Duncan was pointing.

'I thought you had three hives,' said Jim thoughtfully.

'We did,' Duncan replied without batting an eyelid. 'But we merged the two weakest colonies to produce one strong one.' Technically, he was right. Morally, he was in another country.

'Do I qualify for a cut of the harvest?' said Jim after a while. If nothing else, he had done as much as Mr Fowler to get me into beekeeping in the first place by drawing my attention to the swarm in his garden 30 months ago, and by lending me the kit to get started. Since then, he had unwittingly become the annoying parent figure that we always wanted to impress, and a yardstick by which we measured how we were getting on.

'You do,' I replied, pleased to drag the conversation into ethically calmer waters. 'We're taking it on Friday, if you want to join in.' His reply was neutral, but we both knew by now that he would not come. Jim visited only on his own terms.

At that point, Duncan started talking animatedly about the ongoing benefits of our recent registration with Defra, as if it was some cast-iron pointer to our competence and commitment. Clearly this was just an excuse to get away from the tricky subject of Jim's swarm.

The honeybee earns her rest, but is fated never to achieve it.

From dawn till nightfall, she is out foraging. Perhaps she will do twelve or more flights each day, often coming back with her own body weight in nectar and pollen. To do this, her wings adjust for the extra loads like a Formula 1 racing car does, by stretching out her wing stroke amplitude rather than adjusting her wingbeat frequency.[1] In layman's terms, this means that she is never going at anything other than full throttle. There is no human equivalent to this kind of workload, and bees will often die mid-flight, dropping quietly to the ground with shredded wings and their undelivered cargo.

Back in the hive, things are slightly less brutal. The nectar she has gathered will be passed by mouth from bee to bee, each one chewing it for about half an hour until it is ready to be added to the honey cells in the wax foundation. Meanwhile, all that multi-coloured pollen that she has brought in on her back legs is used not to create honey, but as a protein-rich food source for the young bees in the hive. Here, nothing is wasted, and every action has a direct purpose.

Perhaps the most extraordinary part of the whole procedure is the waggle dance, by which returning bees inform their colleagues of the exact direction, distance and quality of food and water sources from the hive. Based on the current angle of the sun, her dance consists of a figure of eight circuit, which she may complete up to 100 times, with an outward 'run' and a backward 'waggle', the direction determined by the angles of the former. Crudely, the further away the target, the longer the waggle; the better the food source, the more energetic the dance. By this device (research into which earned Karl von Frisch a Nobel Prize, by the way), the combined efforts of the colony are made as efficient as they possibly can be.*

Deep in the brood box, the queen is beginning to slow up her egg-laying for the season. At its peak, she has been dropping up to 2,000 each day, but she knows from the gradually shortening days that the priorities of the colony will be changing soon, and that the time of plenty will once again become a time of survival.

The more we learned about our bees, the harder it became for us to remove their honey.

Duncan's spendthrift habits over the previous months had landed us with any number of specialist gadgets that we were fated never to use, but nothing useful like, for example, honey jars.

---

* You would be amazed at the percentage of our beekeeping knowledge that has been gleaned from Wikipedia.

We tried to estimate how much honey we would extract out of the two hives, as it would bear no relation whatsoever to what had gone before. Back then, we were talking about tiny amounts, single figures of jars; now we were looking at industrial quantities. This was our Henry Ford moment, whereby we transferred the whole process to an assembly line. The practised beekeeper knows instinctively how much they are going to end up with, but we were still learners in this respect.

'We need to heft it,' I suggested usefully, mainly because I fancied using the word 'heft'.

I had seen my Alabama apiarist hefting his own hives on YouTube, so I was at least aware that it involved lifting the hive and estimating from the effort required how many bees and how much honey was in it. And because Duncan had wrenched an intercostal muscle heaving a large crate of brassicas into a van a couple of nights before, I agreed to do it myself.

Two minutes later, I had the answer.

'Too bloody heavy,' I told him.

'But how much honey is there? How many jars do we need?'

'Loads.'

Research had told us that each hive would produce some-where between 25 and 60 pounds of honey, depending on the quality of the year and proficiency of the beekeeper. So we averaged out our estimate at 40 pots for each of the two colonies, and then set about manipulating social media to our ends by advertising that a gift of six nice jars would be rewarded by one small pot of Upperfold honey in due course. This gesture, while generous, turned out to be highly effective, and we were soon turning them away. For a reason that I couldn't quite put my finger on at the time, I baulked at the variety of type and size of jar that had been delivered to us, from tiny little samplers to enormous one-litre mayonnaise pots. This time it was me and not Duncan who went mad and bought 96 brand new uniform jars from a local hardware store.

'You can't put that liquid gold in a Hellmann's jar,' I told Duncan, and I could see in his face the unalloyed joy of a messiah who has finally produced a convert.

'Good man,' he said. 'Just one problem. What the hell are we going to do with all the jars we've been given?'

'We'll think of something,' I suggested. But I'm not sure we ever did. The important thing was that we had long since given up trying to keep tabs on our expenditure: we just turned out not to be that sort of beekeeper.

And so it was that we finally hit the jackpot.

After all the false starts, the dead colonies, mishaps and swarms; after sheep up-ending hives, hives disturbing neighbours, and around a dozen stings each; after being the students who couldn't even complete the elementary section of the beekeeping proficiency course, and becoming the dominant contributors to Paynes' 2017 and 2018 profits; after being the buyers of books that had stood unread on our bookshelves, we had finally done it. More through a process of trial and error than education, we had uncorked our tiny river of liquid gold and were free to watch it run.

That August Saturday we spun 44 frames in all. Where the previous summer we made do with a blunt utility knife, this time round we had borrowed a hot electric knife to de-cap the thousands of cells on the frames. For the first time in its young life, our industrial spinner was not so much a ludicrous choice for the job as an effective tool for the amount of honey we were dealing with.

As in the previous year, we tilted the extractor at an angle once we had spun out the honey, opened the tap, and let the precious liquid flow. Pot after pot I held under it, filling each up to a point just underneath its rim before passing it on to Duncan to wipe, and then Caroline to fix the lid. In a world of consistent supermarket food disappointments, this was a treasure beyond price. It was as far from the industrial honey from Brazil or China as could be: this was the distillation of millions upon millions of little local flights, to trees, shrubs and flowers that we saw and walked past every day. These were flights that had physically intersected with our own lives; times when we had been working in the garden and noticed a single bee making its way down a line of lavenders that we had planted the year before, or busying her way across the honeysuckle that rambled over the neighbour's gateway. Each microscopic droplet that now settled in each gleaming new jar was the result of the combined efforts of maybe four or five bees over a two- or three-hour period: aggregated together, it was simply too big to think about. It was also the living proof that when you just let nature get on and do the things that she has been doing since the evolution of the honeybee 30 million years ago, the harvest will come.

And when the harvest came, it was darker than before, and runnier, like late season wild-flower honey is inclined to be. Food straight from nature tends to carry with it more beauty than food that has been processed and adulterated to satisfy the way we live, or the way that supermarkets make more margin, and this was beauty of the highest order. Duncan was right, you could just stare at it for hours; and anyway, staring at things for hours was what Duncan did best in life. Somewhere in a trunk in his attic is a first-class diploma from the Royal College of Staring at Things for Hours.

Caroline, who, despite having had to live for 25 years through the waxing and waning of my various enthusiasms, had persuaded me not only to do this, but to do it well, was as bewitched as we were. What was going on in front of her eyes appealed in equal measure to the scientist, the environmentalist and the artist in her. Secretly, she was also rather delighted that her husband had finally graduated from the University of Short Cuts.

Jar by jar, we stacked up the bounty onto the old table on the terrace, watching the shards of light play through the golden liquid. When there was nothing more to scrape out of the extractor, we sat in the dying rays of the late summer sun, drinking wine and toasting the enterprise.

Excellence doesn't visit my personal parish that often. Here, in the August warmth, we all thought we could hear the soft beating of her wings in the air above, and that was good enough for us.

There on the table were 77 one-pound jars of honey, a full eleven times more than we had managed in our first year. For a time we just sat and admired the pyramid, but we quickly realised that the spinner was attracting the unwanted attention of every unattached wasp in the GU postcode area. Once we had washed and stowed it away, we did what you do when you have created a harvest out of nature's bounty: we toasted three pieces of bread and tasted a sample.

This time, we knew what we were looking for, and we had two previous harvests to compare it with – the dark wildflower honey of last autumn, and the light and crystallised version from the late spring. This was mid-season honey, less dark and sharp than it might have been had we harvested it a few weeks later, but runnier than if it had been June. It had a slight cloudiness to it that meant the pollen had not been filtered out, and layers of flavour, whose complexity stood in sharp contrast to industrially-produced sweeteners. The trick was to shut our eyes as we tasted it, the better to focus on the individual notes within it – grass, clover, borage, for example – and simply to savour each tiny reminder of the trees and flowers around us. I searched in vain for a pot of supermarket honey with whose pasteurised blandness we might compare it, but we no longer kept any.

'I think we need a few more hives next year,' said Duncan. In a way, he meant it. The natural course of action for us now was to get bigger and better, make more honey, create more bees, help pollinate more plants. Three or four hives would be virtually no more work than two, and moreover, they would provide a measure of insurance against the prospect of future disasters. Equally, like me, he didn't want this to be the end of something so much as the beginning of something else. We were both quietly determined to close this particular chapter of our lives not with a full stop, but with a semi-colon;

Chapter 13

THE 77TH ANNUAL
HONEY SHOW

September

....

Being underestimated is one of the
biggest competitive advantages
you can have. Embrace it.
ANON*

....

In my teens, my Dad would reliably open a bottle of vintage port for us every Christmas Eve, when he got back from work. We all have our little ceremonies, and this was his.

....

* Anon clearly didn't go in for honey shows, or he wouldn't have written this garbage.

I remember this principally because of the inordinate care he took to strain it slowly through muslin so that the sediment stayed out of the decanter. It was a ceremony almost beyond the power of speech, as he tipped the bottle slowly ever downwards until the last of the liquid had drained into the filter, and what was left below was brick-red perfection, backlit by the light under the kitchen cupboard. And each year when he had finished, he would pour four tiny glasses of the precious liquid before we went off to Midnight Mass, and we would remark on its excellence, and our hopes that Father Christmas and the coming year would bring us everything we wanted.

As the years went by, he quietly admitted that the bottles were in fact part of a very generous christening present to me from my own godfather, and that he was 'trying to do the right thing' each year by ensuring on my behalf that it hadn't gone off. It hadn't, and it still hadn't when we drained the last bottle of the case just after my 21st birthday.

Thirty-seven years later, I had a vivid flashback to that feeling of not wanting to waste one precious drop in the filtration process, as Duncan, Caroline and I found ourselves one early September Friday night filtering wine-dark wildflower honey through a muslin cloth ourselves, in readiness for the 77th Annual South Downs Honey Show the following weekend.

I'm not entirely sure what possessed us.

By taking that bumper crop of honey, we had already achieved more than we had hoped when we bought the hive, went to the auction, and collected our nuc from Viktor. It was all the justification that was needed for the investment in time, effort and money, and it was completely beside the point that each jar had cost around £15 to bring into this world. Yet the deep underlay of competitiveness that lies beneath the carpet of the male brain tripped us up on our metaphorical route to the larder and said: 'You're better than this, aren't you? Are you too afraid to put your honey forward as the best in the county?' On reflection, we decided that we were, indeed, too afraid to do this, and we moved on. Resistance came from the least expected place, Caroline, who had buried herself in the computer one evening and suddenly called out:

'Two weeks tomorrow. The 77th Annual South Downs Honey Show. Liss Village Hall. Twelve trophies available. Twenty different classes plus four novice classes. You've got to do it.'

Duncan, once he had got over the insulting assumption that he might enter into a novice class, was all ears, and we crowded round the screen to see how we might best plan the campaign.

'No point in entering any competition unless you think you can win it,' I said. 'Class 1J is for juniors between the ages of four and eleven, and is for one pot of honey only.

Raef could do that. After all, he was there all afternoon when we extracted it the first time.'

With regret, we decided that this was not quite in the spirit of the thing, and that our innocent subterfuge would be rumbled as soon as Raef was asked a basic question such as how he had achieved such remarkable clarity in so dark a honey.

'The Janet Jones Memorial Trophy,' said Caroline. 'It's awarded for the highest number of points in the novice class, a novice being defined as someone who has never won a prize at a honey show.'

We thought about it, and decided that we were too old and too clever to be considered juniors or novices, and that we should throw our lot in with the big boys. There would be no Janet Jones Memorial Trophy for us; we were going for the big time, namely the Chichester Trophy for 'the best exhibit of honey in the show in the member, novice and junior classes'. While we weren't entirely sure what it was, we felt that we had something tangible to offer the presiding judge, something that had apparently eluded the many other beekeepers who had been doing this for half a century or more. Ambition like this, after all, is what has driven the ascent of man: from the second he first climbed down from his East African baobab tree and made his way north or east across the savannah, he has been trying to do things that are slightly cleverer than they need to be.

I emailed the Hon. Secretary, who managed to disguise his delight at our enthusiasm.

'The two jars should be the standard honey jars with metal screw on lids. They should be filled just above the bottom of the lid. There should be no honey or residue on the lids. The honey should be clear with no debris or crystallisation present.

Dark is a dark deep brown but not black. If a lighter colour it will be in the next class.

They should have no labels or other markings on the jars just plain and they both need to be the same.

When you deliver them on the Friday evening you will be given two class labels to be fixed at the height of a lid from the bottom.'

This was no village fete produce show. This was the sharp end of the school of hard knocks, where no quarter was asked or given, a kind of special forces selection for local beekeepers where only the very best bubbled to the top and walked off with the silverware. The Hon. Secretary wasn't being unwelcoming; he was simply initiating us into a whole new world of 'who blinks first' excellence, and there was no doubt that Duncan and I would have to be at the top of our game if we were going to get anywhere.

If on a new journey, get a map. That's just a basic life rule.

So I retreated to my desk later in the evening and entered the rather specific search term: 'how to win at honey shows'. The first site I visited blew out of the water any notion that judging would consist of a plump and smiling old lady in a hat and floral print dress dipping her teaspoon into the exhibits and every now and again exclaiming: 'My! That is delicious! Well done, you. And didn't I know your mother?' These judges were made of sterner, more unbending stuff. The website explained that the judge's toolbox would contain a big torch (to look for clarity), a lens or refractometer (to check for foreign bodies), a weighing machine, ruler, tasting rods, and a copy of the schedule and the rules. In the section that applied to us ('preparing liquid honey'), there were no fewer than ten suggestions for how to dress up your offering. We needed to start with a grading glass (to ensure we were entering our honey into the right colour category), and then we had to develop some form of filtration more sophisticated than our big old kitchen sieve. The judge would be looking for any signs of granulation, for bubbles, for pollen, for specks, for hair, for surface-to-air missiles, for almost anything, in fact, aside from the pure monochrome liquid that they wished to inspect. Even the jar selection was problematical. You didn't just bring along your honey in an old Hellmann's jar with the label removed, or a strawberry jam pot that you had just finished two breakfasts ago; no, as the Hon. Secretary had intimated, you brought it in two identical

454-gram jars, with screw-top metallic lids. Finally, you filled the two jars to a line fractionally below the bottom of the lid, and yet you had to keep them vertical all the way to the show, as traces of honey actually on the lid would certainly lose you points. 'Get the jar wrong', said the article ominously, 'and your exhibit will be disqualified without even being opened.' The world we were entering was the countryside's version of Crufts, including the chicanery and subterfuge but minus the problem of what to do if your dog crapped at the wrong time. However bad it was, even our honey couldn't do that.

'We could just go to Waitrose and decant two nice pots of honey for the exhibition,' suggested Duncan. But it turned out they were completely wise to that; these, after all, were true professionals who could tell instantly even if you were trying to fob them off with last year's prize-winning harvest in place of this season's crop; supermarket honey would stick out a mile. Besides, we were proud of what our bees had produced, and wanted the chance to take it into the wider, professional world, even if we face-planted in our efforts.

Thus we started the process of bringing two of our pots up to scratch. Having no sieve finer than the one we had used in the extraction process, we spent an hour and a half the following evening re-straining just one pot's-worth through a butter muslin to see what would happen. We left it overnight and then shone a torch through it in the morning to check for its crystal clarity. We needn't have bothered; if I had read a few lines further on one of the early websites I visited, I would have learned in a rather cheaper way that you should strain through freshly laundered nylon or polyester, as anything else leaves tiny material deposits in the honey. When I shone a torch through the liquid gold, what I actually saw was a kaleidoscope of stationary particles, and the certainty of the exhibiting beekeeper's version of the early bath. The honey looked like a wave looks when it has rolled across a sandy beach.

As with everything we had done hitherto in our journey, the next step was to go and spend more money at Paynes. We had about ten days left, and for the princely sum of £12.60 we bought a nylon double strainer (a third of the price of the steel one), plus next-day post and packaging of £4.95. We then ordered a dozen specialist honey jars (£12.00) from the one supplier on eBay who seemed to be confident of getting them to us by the next afternoon. There was even talk of settling tanks (£42.84) and warming cabinets (£196.99) as well, but this was dangerous talk which, if acted upon, would have propelled us miles over the £1,250 mark in our overall investment. In the end, we rowed back a little on our ambition, and decided that what would be would be: we would exhibit two pots of this season's dark (or probably dark) honey, and the good news was that our researches indicated that dark was the least competitive of the three categories of liquid honey. The real dogfight, it transpired, took place in the medium honey category, and we were pleased that our bees had independently decided to steer us away from it.

Stardom, albeit well disguised stardom, beckoned. And if that worked, we would conquer the whole bloody thing the following year.

I called Viktor. Of course I called Viktor. He knew more about bees than bees did themselves. His advice was unequivocal.

'Don't do it,' he said. 'They are tyrants. It is for them authority. Better to sell honey to the people who like it than show it to the people who criticise it.' He had a point, but I hardly dared to tell him that we were already entered into the show, and were in it up to and beyond our necks.

Once the double nylon filter and twelve jars had arrived, we set aside an evening to do the very best we could for our display honey. Disappointingly, given that it was now two days before judging, the last line of the first section of the instruction ran: 'Once you have completed this, I suggest you leave your jars to settle for a couple of weeks, or even three.' This was much like the recipe for a Christmas cake that you embark on after a couple of sharpeners on Christmas Eve, but which instructs you to leave the dried fruit steeping in the brandy for a couple of weeks. One of our weaknesses as bee farmers lay in our tendency to look at the gist of instructions rather than the whole thing. I think that was the last time we ever got to the final line of anything. After that we stopped reading things altogether.

Fundamentally, there were only three principal challenges: all the foreign bodies needed to be filtered out of the honey; then the residual air bubbles needed to be left for a day or two to rise to the surface where they could be scraped off; and finally the jars needed to be cleaned up to within an inch of their lives for the all-important first impression. This, of course, meant over-filling the pot first time round so that you didn't go below the 'disqualification' line with the actual finished product. The internet was, as usual, either indispensable or completely useless, depending on which way you looked at it.

'I leave mine in the ripening tank overnight,' gushed some well-heeled blogger rather smugly.

'What the hell's a ripening tank?' asked Duncan, and the answer when we dug deeper was a £15 plastic bucket.

'I overfill it and then skim off the bubbles when they have risen to the surface,' said another.

'Carefully press down cling film and then use a teaspoon to get the stuff out of the corners,' said a third. On it went. Page after page after page. Byte after byte from the land of obsession, pearls of wisdom from an unknown continent.

Filtering the honey was even harder, and all the while we were leaving precious liquid in strainers, in sieves, on spoons and on the side of jugs. I reminded Duncan that twelve bees had donated their entire lives' work to make each teaspoon's-worth of honey that we were leaving around, or cleaning up, and all because we were alpha males who wanted to parade our second year of produce and beat the experts at their own game.

By late on Thursday evening, with slightly under 24 hours to let it settle and then find a way of driving it undisturbed the thirteen miles to the venue, we had our exhibitors' pots ready. Sadly, the jars we had specially bought had the green tinge of recycled glass but time had run out by this stage, and we would have to rely on the honey itself being clear, unsullied and delicious once the judges decanted it onto a white plate and inspected it on Saturday morning.

Last thing on Thursday night, I put the three filtered jars on top of the boiler, as someone from an online blog said that was the trick to clarify the honey even further. In 24 hours' time, two of these jars would be out in the big, bad world of competitive honey showing, mixing it through the long night with the other honeys, combs, meads, dressings, cakes, cookies and beeswax that made up the entries, and preparing for the judgment of Solomon the following morning. Or, if not Solomon, a man in a white lab coat with a powerful torch, decades of knowledge and a point to prove.

The law of unintended consequences woke up slightly before I did the following, critical, morning; something it often did.

Before I went to work, I retrieved the jars from the boiler and returned them to the kitchen table, where I could inspect them against the harsh light of the September sun streaming in through the window. What I saw was half-encouraging, in that the honey did indeed seem to be settling with a dark, rich clarity, but half-depressing, in that the heat of the boiler had created another flow of air bubbles which were now resting at, or close to, the surface of the jar. We didn't need to present our products until early in the evening, so I decided to leave them as they were, and then use the old cling film and spoon process just before we drove them over.

By six o'clock it was all sorted, and we climbed into Duncan's pickup with the three jars, from which we would select the best two outside the village hall. We wedged them with tea-towels into a small box and then stuck that between my feet in the passenger footwell, where they stood the best chance of not being rocked around by the motion of the car.

'Does it occur to you that what we are doing is really quite silly?' asked Duncan as he drove westwards through Midhurst. 'I mean, you, Caroline and I between us have spent well over thirty hours in the last week tarting up two pots of honey to enter them into a show. Thirty hours.'

I agreed that it was strange, but that didn't change a thing. What we were doing was also magnificent. We were pitting ourselves against the best beekeepers in Sussex and Hampshire, men and women with decades more experience than us, and there could be no hiding from the consequences.

This was the midlife equivalent of bungee jumping into a New Zealand gorge, or buying a few grams of weed from a dodgy-looking dealer. There would be heroism here, as well, among the scrubbed floorboards and the institutional seating of the village hall.

'Heroism?' asked Duncan. 'Obsessive compulsive disorder, more like. Have you ever been to one of these shows?'

I assured him that I had, and that my grandmother had ruled supreme in the Isle of Mull (South Division) Produce Show for two decades in my youth, and many was the time that I had been press-ganged in to tart up her various offerings so that she could mow up the silverware in her accustomed manner. I knew *exactly* what went on at these events.

We had been so busy reading up about how to get our honey to its best state that we had failed to notice the basic delivery details and arrived in the village a good hour early. A pint later, we were still entering the village hall along with the organisers.

'Are we too early?' I asked.

'Depends what you are here for.' The man looked down at the little box in my hands and agreed that we were, indeed, much too early. They would be an hour of sorting the hall out, and then and only then would the staging begin, that moment where the entries were set up around the room.

'Do you want a hand setting up?' asked Duncan. It was a brazen attempt to curry favour with the entire committee, the ultimate apple for teacher, and I thoroughly approved of it. We introduced ourselves to the Chairman, Secretary, Education Secretary, Treasurer, Membership Secretary and a few others, all the while stressing our childlike enthusiasm and respectfulness. Trestle tables went up around the edge of the hall, followed by a display framework which had to be screwed down, and then the whole thing topped off with long white cloths to give it the desired effect. Hundreds of stacked chairs had to be hidden away, labels put down in front of each exhibit area, and storyboards of the work of the association and the life of the honeybee applied as the backdrop to the staging.

For a second, I looked at it all and mused that all over the country, communities of people were doing things like this, at times like this; esoteric at best, sometimes easy to mock, but nonetheless part of the stitching that holds together the whole tapestry of who we are. Divisive issues could polarise us all they liked; the reality of life is that people will go on coming cheerfully together in the name of the slightly strange things that interest them. The men and women busily setting up the exhibition in the village hall were doing it in their own free time, and because they cared enough. Most of them would not eventually run out winners the following afternoon; they would have just spent happy time with people who were like them, and understood their passions.

By about eight o'clock, we felt confident enough to ask whether we could formally enter our jars and leave them all to it.

'Of course,' said the Hon. Secretary, and gave us a small

label for each jar. As he had previously noted, this had to be precisely affixed at the height of one lid from the bottom of the jar, and equidistant between the two seams that ran down the sides. It was the kind of precision work that Duncan had made his own during the course of our little partnership, and I left him to it. When it was done, we presented them back to the Hon. Secretary with a flourish.

'Two jars of dark, liquid honey,' I said, 'for Class C.'

He looked at it for a second and said: 'That's not dark honey. It's medium. Take a look.' He took a grading glass from his pocket and showed us that we were, indeed, no higher up the medium scale than the middle, and that our exhibit had suddenly been catapulted into the most competitive section in the show. Hiding behind a small handful of specialist entries was no longer an option.

It was the dawning of the truth that we were straight up against the top seeds. This was Roger Federer in the first round, and it was hard to disguise our disappointment.

'Which of you does the actual judging?' asked Duncan, as casually as he could.

'Oh, he's from outside the area,' said the Hon. Secretary. 'We won't see him until judging starts at ten tomorrow morning. Don't forget: results at 4pm precisely.'

Not for the first time, we had just wasted an hour of our lives.

Modesty advised us not to come along on the Saturday until just before the prize-giving. After all, a prize seemed a dead cert for a couple of pots of honey that had cost, cumulatively, the thick end of £300 and taken 30 hours of our recent lives to prepare. And we didn't want to be the sort of people who hung around their starred exhibit looking smug and waiting for passers-by to ask us how we did it. That wasn't how we worked at all. For us it would be the expressions of studied surprise, like the outsider who scoops best supporting actress at the Oscars. 'Oh, my goodness,' we would find ourselves saying. 'I hardly know what to say. Such a surprise. Such an honour.' Such utter bullshit.

So we rolled in at 3.50, just when the prize-giving was getting into its stride. We already knew that the Rita Stilwell Trophy ('the best wax in Class 11') would elude us, as would the Charlie Summersgill Trophy ('best shallow frame in Class 10') and the Lady Grace Trophy ('the best comb honey in Class 8 and 14'). But we weren't greedy. All we wanted was a medal of some sort in the class we had entered, that uber-competitive 'medium liquid honey', and we wouldn't find out whether we had until the bloke with the microphone had stopped talking and we could wander among the exhibits for ourselves, and see what colour card had been posted under our pot.

The extraordinary answer was 'none'. The underside of each of our pots was simply the virginal white of the table-cloth on which they sat.

The red card for first place had been awarded to someone called Brad, the green for second to Tom, and the yellow for third to Graham. Brad came to the table to collect his winning honey, and we wanted to hate both him and it; anyone can nobble a judge if they hang around long enough, and Brad had obviously been knocking around all day, volunteering to go and collect sandwiches, make cups of tea and be generally useful in a room full of people who were already being specifically useful themselves.

'How did you do it?' I asked him through clenched teeth.

'I really don't know. Luck, I suppose,' he replied.

But then I looked at his two jars and, in spite of myself, my ambitions, my hopes, jealousies and prejudices, I had to admit that Brad's honey was in a different class. I was in no way ashamed of mine, but Brad's had a luminous clarity and a rich coloration that made it as perfect as anything I had ever seen since I had started keeping bees. It had no foreign bodies, no bubbles, the correct viscosity, the right percentage of liquid, a powerful nose and a distinctive taste that was as far advanced from ours as ours was from Tesco value honey. From time to time life is unfair, but Brad's gold medal was as justified as any prize I had ever seen awarded. Worse still, he was lovely. Failure, in my experience, does not like to be denied a scapegoat.

Brad patiently explained about the sweet chestnut and borage foraging, the micro extraction of just two frames at a time so that exhibition honey was always separate from the main harvest, and the hours spent with cooling and warming tanks to get the clarity and consistency as near perfect as it could be. He also said that the relentless pursuit of this excellence had blighted his life, and he did not recommend we take it up.

'Once you start it,' he said, 'you find that you can't stop. Occasional becomes regular. Local becomes national. Every weekend, it's the same thing, and it just takes over your life.'

When he had gone, and everyone in the hall was busily deconstructing the displays and packing the honeys, meads, waxes and combs away into their antique wooden boxes, Duncan and I stood for a while and took in the scene. We had come a long way in the seventeen months since we had started keeping bees, and we knew we wanted to progress further. However, we promised each other there and then that there would be no more time-consuming shows: that was not at all why we were in the game. People like Brad, Tom and Graham won prizes because they were utterly dedicated to the craft of apiculture, and it would be years, decades even, before we were fit to lick their competitive boots. Duncan was happy to continue as we had started, in our own sweet haphazard way; for my part, I had met enough niceness and helpfulness here to want a little more of it and, in spite of myself, it took me a few more days to decide not to join the club. My worry was that not joining would prevent me from tapping into a rich vein of honey gossip.

When we were leaving, we saw that the judge had written out a little note in his book against Exhibit Class B 001: 'Certainly not put to shame.' It was like one of those short descriptions that they put against the name of the worst horse of the day in the race-card at the local meeting: 'The company may be a bit above her today.' But it was fine for us.

Not put to shame. That was progress enough for Phase One. That was almost something that we could report back to Jim.

Almost.

As we walked out into the late September afternoon, we told each other not to be disappointed but, in a way, it was impossible not to be. Poor innocents that we were in the brutal world of competitive apiculture, we had put our hearts and souls into the competition, and we had been ever so gently reminded where we were in the hierarchy of excellence. Anchored about two rungs up from the ground, that's where we were.

We collected up our precious pots of honey rather than donating them to the club, as we had been encouraged to, for its annual sale of produce.

'We've only got another four,' Duncan lied to the lady on the door as he was caught sneaking our harvest of dreams out of the hall and back into his pickup. She smiled at him and said that she understood, but in a way that suggested she didn't. And that it took all sorts. And that he was tighter than a duck's arse.

'Quick one?' he asked, looking wistfully towards the beer garden of the nearby pub.

There was a *fin de siècle* feel about the moment, and I agreed that we needed to mark it with something stronger than the tepid contents of the flask of tea we had brought along.

'We're not very good at joining in with things, are we?' I observed, after we had sat down. 'Beekeepers' associations, for example. Lessons. Competitions. Apart from Defra, of course.'

'Depends what you want out of it, mate,' he said. 'Personally, I just want to get slowly better so that I can enjoy it as I go along, and teach my boys when they're old enough. I know I could learn faster, and be better quicker, but …' He left the sentence unfinished, but I knew what he meant, because it was what I felt too.

Our adventure was about many things, and we didn't want to get carried away and short-circuit it.

Yes, it was about the plight of the honeybee, and working in harmony with nature; it was about immersing ourselves in a brand-new mysterious world, and of understanding how to be better at it. It was about the myriad different colours of pollen on the panniers of the foraging bees coming back to the hive on a spring evening, and the way that bees could only think collectively, not individually. It was about the curls of woodsmoke rising up into the summer air from the smoker, and the blocks of fondant that were our own down-payment to the bees in return for their honey when the weather got bitter. It was about the faint smell of antihistamine gel on the welt of each sting.

It was, for a fraction of a moment in time, to cup an ear to a sound other than a manufactured one, and to hear instead the gentle voice of a bruised planet.

It was as small as each tiny hexagonal cell that was filled by the bees with honey or brood, or as large as the 50,000 or so trees and plants within the three-mile radius that they could forage. It was about the slow, slow flow of liquid gold into each pristine one-pound jar, and the perfection of a piece of toast smothered with random brace comb. It was a time of adventure and misadventure, and the gradual dawning of knowledge. At a time of challenges and discord in the news, it was just a useful and harmonious activity that helped to make the world a fractionally better place. It was about the many people who walked alongside us and enjoyed it too. It was about the person I was yet to become, and the way that relying on nature had allowed me to identify who he was.

But, maybe above everything else, it was about what the Australians call 'mateship', that irreplaceable 'band of brothers' sense when two people do some shared thing, be it ever so slightly crazy, together. In a world where it has never been easier to communicate *at* each other across the ether, what we had been doing over the last year and a half was communicating *with* each other over our bees. From not even knowing each other eighteen months before, we had forged a close but uncomplicated friendship based on stuff that was going on in two medium-sized white boxes in a far corner of my paddock.

Two medium-sized white boxes in the corner of a paddock that hosted a hundred thousand beating hearts of effort and endeavour, and that helped us understand a little bit more the countless billions of interconnections of the hidden natural world around us.

And we had only just started.

Epilogue

THE PLIGHT OF
THE BEE, AND HOW
YOU CAN HELP

....

*You may not control all the events
that happen to you, but you can
decide not to be reduced by them.*
MAYA ANGELOU

....

The bee is a better friend to us than we can possibly imagine.

For this reason, our story should not just come to a convenient full stop in the autumn sunshine outside that village hall, with two delusional beekeepers and their near-perfect jars of medium liquid honey. There is quite a big 'so what' to all this.

When you see that lone honeybee on the lavender in the window box of your flat, or that bumblebee droning around the daisies on your lawn, your life is for one tiny moment intersecting with one of the 100 billion or so daily journeys that bees make up and down the land, the by-product of which is to pollinate the plant life around us, and thus enable nature to sustain us all.

As with much of the natural world, man's recent effect on bee populations and welfare has not generally been a happy one, and there have been declines right across the species. But there are also acres of light at the end of this tunnel, so our story ends instead with how easy it is to make a direct and significant difference to the plight of the bee.

Perhaps we need to start with a few boring facts.

There are 250 species of bee in the UK: 25 species of bumblebee, 224 species of solitary bee and one honeybee species. Between them, they make up about 15% of the 1,500 or so insect types that pollinate our plants for us, but only just over 1% of the 20,000 bee species worldwide.[1] There are at present around 250,000 working hives in the UK, spread out among 44,000 beekeepers and 200 commercial bee farmers,[2] which might mean around a billion domesticated bees in all. No one knows how many wild colonies can be added to this, and it is a declining number, but the vast quantities of bees can give the mistaken impression of a thriving species. Actually, one way or another, their numbers have been in consistent decline since the 1980s.

In March 2015, a report set out in stark terms that over 9% of European wild bee species were threatened with extinction, and a further 5% are threatened in the near future.[3] Aggregated, the work of bees and other pollinators adds approximately £700 million per year to the value of UK crops through increased yield, work that would somehow need to be originated by humans in the absence of bees.[4] In terms of biodiversity, there has been an overall decline of 13% between 1980 and 2014[5] which, even by man's standards, is some going.

The various causes for this decline are hotly debated, and a small-time beekeeper from West Sussex with zero scientific knowledge is not about to add usefully to the debate. However, experts seem to agree on the following menu of four areas where things have gone wrong for them:

1. Habitat loss, arising from changes in agricultural use and urbanisation, particularly the loss of flower-rich habitat.
2. Pesticides, especially neonicotinoids.*
3. Disease, especially the Varroa mite viruses back in the 1990s.
4. Climate change. Warmer and wetter winters disrupt nesting behaviour and lead to bees being in the wrong place at the wrong time.

....

* The effect of neonicotinoids on honeybees is still a hotly debated topic, and my advice is to read from both sides of the scientific argument if you are interested in further research.

The better news is that, in recent years, the rate of decline seems to have stabilised somewhat alongside deliberate planned changes in human behaviour. In November 2014, the UK government set out its National Pollinator Strategy which, while not necessarily an easy read, actually sets out a clear direction and a series of policy actions. And the best news of all is that there is a whole raft of things that we can do as individuals to reverse the trend completely.

There are about 28 million households in the UK, and from halls to high-rise blocks, there are very few of them which cannot actively contribute to the welfare of the honeybee if they choose to. And every act of environmental helpfulness is so much more effective when multiplied by 28 million, especially when a sizeable proportion of them are done by children, who can build practically on their youthful fascination for the next 70 or 80 years. After all, my bee-keeping 'career' started when I was a nine-year-old boy with Mr Fowler back in the late 1960s, even if nothing much happened for nearly half a century afterwards. Also, by and large, any action you take on behalf of the honeybee will be helpful to all the other species of bee as well.

Twelve actions you can take, easiest first:

1. *Teach children to respect bees, and not swat them.* A bee will only sting if it feels threatened, or if it feels its honey stores are under attack. A foraging bee doing its stuff around your garden or the margins of the local

woodland is busy and peace-loving, and has no reason to attack anyone. Perhaps the best thing we can do for bees and all other wildlife is to educate the next generation about the awe and wonder that surrounds them, as well as give them an understanding that the natural world is what we depend upon. The skills of the naturalist are being lost at a time when we need them the most – to document, record and monitor the world, as well as put practical action into place. Learning to know, understand and respect natural history at home and in school is a very good place to start. Respectful children grow into useful adults.

2. *Forget pesticides*. Just rule them out of your life altogether, and remember that their job is simply and solely to kill things, including insects, and therefore bees. There are alternative treatments as simple as good hygiene or watering the soil and not the leaves, or as complex as disguising the smell of, for example, a carrot from a carrot fly. The Pesticide Action Network (www.pan-uk. org) has an excellent section on gardening without pesticides. Then go off and read Rachel Carson's book *Silent Spring*, and allow your heart to soar with how far we have come already.

3. *Don't obsess about weeding*. Weeds are generally not just not a bad thing, but a good thing. They provide a haven for honeybees and other pollinators, an important food

source when other supplies may be running short. Many of them are a sign of healthy soil. If you really want to get rid of weeds that don't fit in, or are highly invasive, then try to pull and dig them up instead of poisoning them. And leave the ivy where it is.

4. *Contact your local beekeeping association if you find a swarm in your garden*, which will only happen in the spring or early summer. Do not try to disperse them by spraying them with a hose or waving things at them: they are probably desperately hungry, very peaceful and just there while their scouts are looking for a new home.* A beekeeping association will be glad to take the swarm: they might charge you a nominal amount, or just remove it for the price of a cup of tea, but that swarm will live to fight another day, and become another colony. The British Beekeepers Association website (www.bbka.org.uk) has a postcode service where you can contact your nearest expert. It's a good thing to have the number down where it is accessible quickly, as a swarm will arrive in your garden with no warning.

5. *Buy local honey*. It sounds too simple, but by buying local honey, you will be directly supporting a local bee-keeper, and directly encouraging them by your demand

....

* According to the NBU, the chances of a swarm surviving in the wild in the UK these days are under 40%.

to take on more hives, and so increase the population. Unlike mass-produced supermarket honey, which has had much of the natural goodness pasteurised out of it, you will benefit from one of earth's most natural products. And honey from the land around you will be full of anti-allergens to help you cope with hay fever and other allergies, although it is fair to say that some doctors and scientists would consider this unproven. Besides, it is likely that only 10% of the honey consumed in the UK actually comes from the UK in the first place, a phenomenon that should be borne in mind by all consumers buying a pot with a picture of an idyllic English garden scene on the label.

6. *Buy local, organic food where you can.* Buying locally means eating seasonally and without damaging food miles. Admittedly, this is much easier in the summer, but good organic box schemes run twelve months of the year. And because you are supporting farmers who are growing without the help of pesticides, you will encourage more of them to come into the business. And no, they are not more expensive. Since we have been subscribing to an organic box scheme, we have found both food bills and wastage rates have declined.

7. *Leave some water around for the bees.* You would not automatically know that every species of bee dehydrates just as any human being does, but they do. Often, when

you see a fat and listless bumblebee seemingly stuck somewhere, this will be the problem. She is dying, and you can save her. While bees will naturally take on water from the dew on the grass, or from a wet flower, it is not always possible. Leaving something as simple as a bowl of water lying around (and remembering to refill it) is a small generosity for which you will be amply rewarded. Make sure the bowl has gently sloping sides, so that bees can walk out safely.

8. *Make or buy a beehouse*. You can get these nowadays at most garden centres, although they are quite easy to make with a few small bamboo canes (maximum gap should be well under 1cm) and some kind of framework. These will provide a home for solitary bees, who tend to be very much more effective pollinators than honeybees. There is no limit as to how ambitious these structures can be, but a few small ones strategically placed around the outside of the house and the garden will make a surprising difference. The simplest ones are well under £10, and even the most elaborate seldom venture much above £25. You could also join the Bumblebee Conservation Trust and become an activist in the battle to make things better for them: https://www.bumblebeeconservation.org/join/

9. *Don't cut down ivy*. Everyone seems to hate ivy, for the destructive effect it can have on masonry and on trees. However, young ivy does no damage at all, and it hosts

blossom that lives on deep into the winter and is often the last source of natural food for a bee long after everything else has gone. Just walk past an ivy hedge in December, and you will see what I mean, so leave it where it is.

10. *Plant a wildlife garden.* Or, at least, a little space for wildlife within the rest of your garden. If you are lucky enough to have some spare space, there is no end of things you can do to encourage bees, but this is also where the hard work begins. As a rule, the easier a plant is (e.g. annuals and bedding plants) the less good it is for a bee. A variety of plants with different sized flowers is best, as different bees have different lengths of tongue. For flowers, go for the old cottage garden favourites, like columbine, larkspur and pinks; Friends of the Earth (www.friendsoftheearth. uk) sell bee-friendly seed mix, as do many others. For shrubs, the list is endless: ceanothus, heather, thyme, blackthorn, bramble, and lilac to name but a few. There is a really good information section on this on www.helpthe honeybee.co.uk. As a rule of thumb, bees tend to go for the colours blue, purple and yellow. Just as anything you do for the honeybee will be good for its cousins, so anything you do for bees in your garden will look beautiful and encourage other wildlife too. Finally, put in a fruit tree or two.

11. *Stagger seasonal planting.* People new to gardening sometimes make the mistake of planning everything to

arrive at the same time. When this happens, your local bees will suffer from feast and famine, particularly in the 'June gap' when the blossom has largely finished and most of the flowers haven't yet come out. Any decent garden centre will be able to advise you on how to stagger your planting so as to keep your bees happy for six months, rather than six weeks.

12. *Become a beekeeper.* No, really. Becoming a beekeeper, be it on ever such a small scale, is the biggest single thing you can do to halt the decline of the bee population. The chances are that you are more competent and less easily distracted than Duncan and I have been, and the quality of the outcomes is very closely related to the quality of the input. Once you have established yourself with the kit* and the basic knowledge, it will become a hobby that can take up as little or as much of your time as you choose: fifteen to twenty minutes per week in the summer is probably the bare minimum to concentrate on queen management and swarm control, and beyond that it is just basic good animal husbandry and hygiene.

....

* This by no means needs to be ruinously expensive. You and your bees have no idea to start with if you are going to like each other, so a second-hand hive and some kit off eBay need only set you back, say £100 or so, while you are finding out. You need to be careful where second-hand kit comes from, however, as it can well harbour disease, disabling your new colony before you have even started. Bees will either be free (a gift or a swarm) or between £50 and £150.

I have seen hives on balconies high up in tower blocks in London, and on frozen chalet roofs in the Alps; I have seen serried ranks of them behind hedges in Oxfordshire, and tiny little skeps outside a Scottish sitting room window. There are a thousand sources of information and instruction available to you at the click of a mouse on a search bar, and probably dozens of slightly obsessed people in your vicinity who would love to take you under their wing and walk you through your first, tentative baby steps. I can only say that the very first taste of your very own honey is an experience beyond description, and well worth everything you put into it. Despite my own experience on a beekeeping course, most practised beekeepers will rightly say that the best thing a new enthusiast can do is to enrol on, and complete, a short winter course before ever touching a bee or buying any kit at all. Abandoned hives from short-term enthusiasts leave distressed bees and annoyed neighbourhoods, so don't assume at the start that it will inevitably work for you.

Also, let politicians know what you think. The laziest thing in the world is to say that voting changes nothing, and that all politicians are in it for themselves. Most of them want to make the world a better place too, and can be galvanised into action by the volume and intensity of your support.

When all is said and done, the bee was here 30 million years before you and I were, and our successors need her still to be here long after we have gone. For most of those years she, for it is dominantly 'she', has just got on with things alongside the rhythms of the seasons and whatever nature provides her with, and it is only since the agricultural revolution that she has suffered at the hands of man.

Since 1962, bees have increasingly been used as bio-indicators in various surveys to monitor environmental pollution.[6] There are two ways in which they perform this function, one of which lies in the residues in the honey they produce, the other in their own rates of mortality. One of the things that bees have been able to point out scientifically through their own suffering is the 'molecular contamination' (a euphemism for poisoning) brought about by pesticides, the biggest damage of course being done by the market leaders. Farmers and gardeners are much more aware of this danger than they were back in the last century, and many have tried to adjust their behaviour accordingly, but lazy industrial practices still continue in many parts of the world, including ours.

If you are inspired by this book to take one personal step, then you could make a pledge never to use a single non-organic pesticide or herbicide again in your life. And if there is one more thing that you are happy to do, make the space around you, however small it happens to be, bee-friendly.

GLOSSARY OF TERMS

(... or those not explained in the text)

Anaphylaxis: Nature's way of telling you that you shouldn't be a beekeeper. Anything of which 'death' is listed as a possible side-effect should give even the most heroic enthusiasts pause for thought.

Bee space: The 3/8ths of an inch that a bee needs to crawl between two things, unless one of those things happens to be an Asian hornet.

Biodiversity: The total variety of all the plant and animal life in a specific area or habitat. Monoculture (qv) has been a surprisingly clever way of reducing it.

Biomass: The total weight of organisms in a given area. Forty thousand bees being closely inspected by Duncan have a biomass of 98kg.

Brood box: The bottom bit of the hive in whose eleven frames all the egg-laying gets done, and where all the swarming and general misbehaviour is planned.

Capped cells: The waxy substance with which the bee seals up a cell full of brood or honey in the vain hope that it will still be there after September.

Colony: The contents of one hive, if owned, or one tree cavity, if not.

Comb: A block of filled hexagonal wax cells which allows beekeepers to offer a tempting alternative to liquid honey, and Home County delis to charge a king's ransom.

Crown board: The thin plywood covering to the top frame of the hive, above which all looks calm and ordered, and below which mayhem normally reigns.

Drone: A male honeybee, and the living proof that a life of sex and living off others isn't all it's cracked up to be.

Foundation: A wax plate which acts as a shortcut for bees building comb, and one of the few really helpful things that man has done for honeybees.

Frame: The wooden construction into which the foundation wax is placed and on which the bees operate, or not, as the mood takes them.

Herbicide: A method of killing off a small amount of unwanted vegetation, and a large amount of unwanted insects.

Honey super: Any one of three or four boxes above the brood box (qv), and whose very visible number tends also to be the secret currency of beekeeper one-upmanship.

Mating flight: The single journey that most queens make is to a drone congregation area to get impregnated with enough sperm for two million eggs, and which causes enough male suffering to satisfy even the most ardent feminist.

Mesh floor: A boxed screen below the lowest box in the hive, which acts as ventilation, on the one hand, and a downhill Varroa theme park ride, on the other. Also, a useful place to lose car keys.

Monoculture: The agricultural equivalent of economies of scale, in which the farmer concentrates on the most profitable crop, and as a result of which the bee eventually goes elsewhere, if there still is an elsewhere.

Moveable frame hives: Pastor Langstroth's huge contribution to apiculture and bee welfare, which meant that bees could be regularly inspected, and honey taken, without destroying or disrupting the hive.

Nectar: A sweet fluid secreted by plants to tempt insects to provide a pollination service.

Pesticide: Man's foolproof way of killing off enough insects to ensure that car windscreens remain nice and clean on long journeys.

Pheromones: External chemical secretions that influence the behaviour of honeybees.

Pollen: The male bit of plant breeding whose ferrying around the place also happens to be the price a foraging bee pays for her nectar.

Pollinators: Any insect, bird or animal who helps move pollen around for the furtherance of plant life, and whose possible future absence would cost over £1 billion to replicate.

Predator: Anything that attacks and eats a bee, from swifts, martins and thrushes, through wasps and hornets and all the way to my exceptionally unintelligent junior Jack Russell.

Propolis: Sticky when hot, hard when cool, propolis is the bee's equivalent of insulation double glazing, only without the annoying cold-calling beforehand.

Queen excluder: The thin mesh layer between two boxes that allows anyone but the queen to pass through, and should mean that your honey isn't full of bee larvae at breakfast.

Queen: The engine room of hive reproduction and the only fertile bee in the colony. Does exactly what she is told in return for being endlessly fed and cleaned around.

Re-queening: Replacing a troublesome queen with a new one while no one is looking. Possibly the nearest human equivalent is Mary, Queen of Scots.

Skep: An ancient upturned kind of wickerwork laundry basket onto whose inner surface the honeybee theoretically creates comb. Also, a useful crossword clue, or Scrabble word.

Worker: A female honeybee, and possibly the best advertisement in nature for an early retirement policy.

ACKNOWLEDGEMENTS

The author's name on the front cover of any book is only the tip of a large, creative iceberg, and I have been overwhelmed by the help from others that I have received in writing *Liquid Gold*.

Bees engender strong feelings of protection in right-thinking people, just as books about them engender advice and support in equal measure. I am very indebted to the following:

Viktor Zaichenko (Honey Bee Supplies, Hook Norton) for endless advice, cheerful opinions and some very high-quality bees.

Nicholas Brading (Master beekeeper, North Yorkshire), who kindly double-checked the manuscript for bee-accuracy, and suggested improvements.

Roderic Robertson, Tim Hill and John Fielder, all of whom provided local bee-advice when we were very green and naive.

Dave Goulson, author of *A Sting in the Tale*, for helpful suggestions for the Epilogue.

My agent, Clare Grist Taylor, who believed in the project wholeheartedly from Day 1, and knew where best to take it.

Duncan Heath of Icon Books, for having faith in both writer and book from the day he saw it, and editing it himself sensitively and cleverly.

The rest of the team from Icon Books – Andrew Furlow, Victoria Reed, Ruth Killick, Lucy Cooper, Ellen Conlon, Robert Sharman – for being a joy to work with.

Carla, Arthur, Marie, Roland and Lynne, my immediate neighbours, for putting up with my 100,000 or so little tenants crawling all over their gardens.

Duncan, for being happy to let his reputation be hung out to dry in public.

And my wife, Caroline, for once again letting an enthusiasm run its complete course.

NOTES

Chapter 5

1. N. and G. Koeniger, 2007. 'Mating flight duration of *Apis mellifera* queens', *Apidologie*, 38(6), pp 606–11.
2. David Gilmour, *The Pursuit of Italy*.

Chapter 6

1. *Collective Thermoregulation in Bee Clusters*. The Royal Society, 2014. Worth a read.

Chapter 7

1. Professor Ratnieks and Mihail Garbuzov, University of Brighton.

Chapter 8

1. 'Lost traditions of the Sacred Bee'. *Atlantis Rising Magazine*.
2. Royal Holloway, University of London.
3. University of Illinois, 2011. Except the last bit. Obviously.

Chapter 9

1. Office of National Statistics. Interestingly, this is roughly the same as are killed by dogs and by terrorists, but five more than are killed by rats.

Chapter 10

1. Separate adventures described in earlier books *Not Out First Ball* and *Unlimited Overs*.

Chapter 11

1. *Buzz* (Thor Hanson, Icon Books, 2018). A readable and highly informative account if you want to know a great deal more about bees, who they are, and how they work.

Chapter 12

1. Live Science, 2006. 'Scientists finally figure out how bees fly'.

Epilogue

1. House of Commons report on the UK bee population, November 2017.
2. National Bee Unit database, 2016.
3. European Commission press release, March 2015.
4. Supporting document to National Pollinator Strategy, November 2014.
5. UK biodiversity indicators, 2017.
6. *Bulletin of Insectology*, Number 56, 2003; Giorgio Celli and Bettina Maccagnani.